The Teacher Within
A Voyage of Discovery

D. Cecil Clark

Copyright © 2000 by D. Cecil Clark
All rights reserved.

No part of this book may be reproduced in any form whatsoever, whether by graphic, visual, electronic, filming, microfilming, tape recording, or any other means, without written permission of the author, except in the case of brief passages embodied in critical reviews and articles where the author, title and ISBN are mentioned.

This book is not an official publication of The Church of Jesus Christ of Latter-day Saints. All opinions expressed herein are the author's and are not necessarily those of the publisher or of The Church of Jesus Christ of Latter-day Saints.

Published and Distributed by:

Granite Publishing and Distribution, L.L.C.
868 North 1430 West • Orem, Utah 84057
(801) 229-9023 • Toll Free (800) 574-5779
FAX (801) 229-1924

First Printing, July 2000

Cover Photo by:
Cover Design by: Tamara Ingram
Page Layout and Design by:

Library of Congress Catalog Card Number: 00-105998
ISBN : 1-930980-03-5

THE TEACHER WITHIN

A Voyage of Discovery

D. Cecil Clark

Table of Contents

Foreword i

Introduction iii

Chapter 1: Fundamentals Of Teaching Expressed 1
           Through Church Materials

Chapter 2: The Inner Self 5

Chapter 3: Studying Your Teaching 33

Chapter 4: Methods For Studying Your Teaching 45

Chapter 5: Studying Other Teachers 61

Chapter 6: Teacher Beliefs 91

Chapter 7: Gospel Study 107

Chapter 8: Preparing A Lesson 123

Chapter 9: Teaching With The Spirit 145

Chapter 10: Those Who Work With Teachers 151

Afterword 157

Appendix 159

A special thank you to
Warren and Tricia Osborn
for the use of their study for
the book cover and to
John Allen Jones
cover model

FOREWORD

This book is not about teaching, but about you and me as teachers. No longer can we think of "teaching" as a bagful of disembodied methods being applied by a teacher in a classroom. It is much too complex for that. Teaching is an immensely human activity, very much involving the teacher's inner self, the "soil from which good teaching comes." And by looking at our teaching selves at work in a specific classroom, we can know where our development must lie.

The title *The Teacher Within* carries double meaning. First, we teach who we are and cannot help but do so. The inner self permeates every aspect of our teaching. Second, the teacher within each of us can, with help from the Spirit, become our mentor for our own improvement.

I write to salute the hundreds of tireless, courageous and often trembling teachers who, day in and out, go before students, fulfilling their stewardships. Some go with dry mouth, perspiring body, hives, and internal tension. Others soar and dip on emotional roller coasters as they blaze through scriptures, comments and class discussions, energized by it all. Still others are relaxed and confident, warmly satisfied with the day's endeavors. Few, but fortunately not many, are delighted by their cavalier performance before a forbearing audience. In all, these are teachers in the Church who have been called to bless the lives of their students.

But there is a larger purpose in my writing. President David O. McKay, many years ago, laid it clearly before us: "No greater responsibility can rest upon any than to be a teacher of God's children."[1] Elder Dallin H. Oaks, in a General Conference address 46 years later, confirmed the purpose of our church teaching: "We want everyone to have great gospel teachers, and we want those teachers to help all of us find our way back, not just to them [great teachers] but to our Heavenly Father."[2]

I call you to a higher level in your *continuing* development as a teacher, a level which opens up new possibilities—a voyage of discovery. Those fundamental principles of teaching you have learned through teacher development programs and through unending trial and error will be expanded and enlarged as you discover new ways of thinking about your teaching, your inner self as it finds expression in your teaching, and you as student of your teaching.

While I have endeavored with this book to harmonize with counsel from the Brethren and with Church-sponsored materials, the book has received no recognition or official support. Its concepts and possibilities have developed from my research, observations and work with Church teachers and their teaching over the past 30 years. I assume sole responsibility for any faulty thinking, misdirection, undue emphasis and downright error.

Though I desire to be helpful to the valiant teachers of the Church, I admit to an additional, less altruistic motive: Teaching is in my bones. I relish those infrequent moments when my students and I stumble upon a new awareness, a new insight, a simple truth. I also relish the fascinating complexity of teaching, especially within the most interesting of all places: the Church culture. Studying it has been an irresistible passion. My wife has often warned me about the long-term perils of sitting through Sunday School classes making observational notes rather than opening my scriptures for my own salvation.

Attempting the improbable, I write to both the newly-minted teacher and the seasoned veteran. A personal style seems most appropriate—we might well be engaged in a leisurely conversation at the close of an in-service meeting.

As with my earlier book, I am indebted to Sharon Black for her unrelenting precision and creative revising in editing, and to Rebecca Rocque for her excellent layout and formatting of the manuscript. My thanks also go to Debra Taylor, Gaile Clark, Nysje Baker, Gary Beckstead, Lee Donaldson, David Mills and Kevin Bulloch for their willing and careful reading of the text for content and tone.

[1]David O. McKay, *Gospel Ideals*, 1953, p. 175.
[2]Dallin H. Oaks, "Gospel Teaching." *Ensign*, November 1999, p. 78.

INTRODUCTION

On His Errand

This book is anchored in a significant theme: In teaching, we are on His errand not our own. We are different people in a classroom when we are teaching for the Lord than when we are speaking for ourselves. In both circumstances we retain our personal identity, but our motives are different. Selflessness characterizes pure Gospel service; self interest peeks through when we forget the purpose of our teaching and the source of our inspiration. Usually we are a mixture of the two: pure intentions, with humanness popping out here and there. Our desires to be single minded bump into our needs to be recognized and accepted. But we are patient with ourselves. For some of us, years are required before we can go before students with untangled agendas, with no other purpose than to bless lives. If you were born with other-centeredness, your teaching life is easier. Most of us go through maturing phases as teachers, phases which parallel our personal development. Through daily repentance and development of Christ-like attributes, our teaching becomes less muddled with our own weaknesses and more open to the needs of our students.

We become able to carry out His errand, which is, at a fundamental level, to invite souls to Christ, in a myriad of ways: a prayer, a final run through notes, a giving of self, an example, a smile, an expression of caring, a sharing of insight, a bearing of testimony, a phone call, a visit. We carry the message: We *teach* in His stead.

How easy to conclude, on frustrating days, that our calling is misplaced. Definitely Sister Hansen or Brother Pinder would be superior in teaching this class. More frightening is the thought that we are the Lord's best at this moment, all He has to work with until someone more qualified comes along. But we underestimate ourselves. When the call comes to teach—whether hurriedly issued in the hall or deliberately extended in the bishop's office—we accept with assurance that the Lord wants *us* here and now. Our faith provides the determination; He will magnify through our diligence.

No teacher I have interviewed has seen teaching as unimportant. That is because we all know it to be a way of bringing others to

Christ. Teaching is a form of soul making. Our leaders have instructed us of its importance:

> Effective teaching is the very essence of leadership in the Church.[1]
>
> Every member needs a friend, a responsibility and *to be nourished by the good word of God* [italics added].[2]
>
> But it does seem to me that, next to the home, the destiny of the young people of this Church is shaped within the sound of your voice in the classrooms. And that is a very sobering responsibility.[3]

In 1999, the First Presidency called on all "to revitalize and improve teaching in the Church." This call is "intended to improve gospel teaching in homes and in Church meetings and help nourish members with the good word of God."[4]

If we can subscribe to this real purpose of Church teaching, the concepts encountered in this book will have a truer ring and will have relevance to our work in classrooms.

A Call To Raise The Bar

Overall, the picture for quality teaching is brighter than it has been; yet the quality of teaching in the Church can still improve:

> Effective as we have been we can become much more effective.[5]
>
> We must do a better job teaching. The core of our meetings is teaching.[6]
>
> There is a need "to revitalize and improve teaching in the Church."[7]
>
> Some may wonder why we are making such an extensive effort to improve gospel teaching. Those who wonder

must be blessed with superior teachers, and we have many of those in the Church. Others will understand why such an effort is needed and will pray for its success . . . . Notwithstanding the great examples [of good teaching] I have observed, I am convinced that in the Church as a whole—as with each of us individually—we can always do better.[8]

How do these admonitions translate into our individual teaching lives? Our youth and teenagers are growing in sophistication, and our adults are strengthening their gospel scholarship. Concurrently, the numbers of those inexperienced in the gospel are growing. Improved teaching is needed for both experienced and inexperienced—to deepen understanding and provide a foundation. This is a tall order. Fundamental skills must be developed and refined into competent and, wherever possible, excellent skills. No longer can a teacher spend the entire class period reviewing what students already know and have known for years. No longer can a teacher get through an entire lesson without introducing at least one new insight or concept. No longer can a teacher be content in having students take turns reading scriptures for forty minutes. No longer can teachers of youth substitute personality for Gospel substance. No longer can high priest instructors stroll in with fifteen minutes of preparation, nor can elders quorum instructors speak glibly without serious gospel scholarship. Sunday School teachers who are called to teach the youth can no longer prepare their lessons during Priesthood or Relief Society meetings. Teachers in the Primary can no longer bring teenage sons or daughters to entertain as a way of compensating for inadequate preparation. Threadbare lessons can never lead to serious classroom thinking until those who teach deepen their own gospel roots. Renewed commitment, planning, and effort are critical; so also is a growing maturity and effectiveness among already adequate and already good teachers.

Every teacher is urged to study and apply fundamental principles of teaching that have been identified by the Brethren and disseminated in Church materials on teacher improvement. This book is designed to help the teacher *unfold and translate* these principles into everyday teaching life. They serve as a common ground to begin our journey. Firmly moored, then, we move forward. In two earlier books on Church teaching[9] my attempts to integrate a sensitive rendering of secular knowledge with spiritual knowledge lacked integration, were incomplete, and out-of-balance. The spiritual would seldom shed light on the secular, and the secular seemed irrelevant to the spiritual. The books ended up in two parts: oil and water. But unremittingly, I believe that combining truth from the spiritual and knowledge from the secular will lead to a more productive approach to teacher *development* than knowledge from either source alone.

The journey is undertaken from the following premise: *Who one is and how one teaches are dynamically related. Method is the instrument through which the inner self is expressed. Maximal improvement comes by increasing goodness and by the study of your teaching.* The "inner self" is who we are inside: our core, our spiritual and emotional make-up, our fears, hopes and ambitions—our person-ness. "The study of your teaching" includes whatever occurs in your classroom: lecturing or answering questions, students commenting, every one laughing, the group discussing, an outline being followed, personal experiences being shared, testimonies being expressed. For help in increasing goodness of the inner self, we can turn to spiritual truths; for help in improving efforts in your classroom, we can, in addition, profit from secular knowledge.

The journey begins with a summarization of the principles of teaching expressed through Church materials. We move immediately to the inner self and see how repentance brings fundamental changes to one's teaching. Then we see how expanding the teacher's awareness of his or her teaching opens new possibilities for growth, guided by the Spirit and the inner self. Methods are offered to help the teacher increase awareness of events in his or her own teaching as well as that of others. Next, we consider teacher beliefs that both impede and facilitate growth. We move on to studying the Gospel, preparing a lesson, teaching with the Spirit; finally, we shift the perspective to considering possibilities for those who work with teachers.

[1]President Gordon B. Hinckley, General Authority Priesthood Board Meeting, 5 February, 1969.
[2]President Gordon B. Hinckley.
[3]Elder Neal A. Maxwell.

⁴Letter to all wards from the First Presidency, September 15, 1999.
⁵President Gordon B. Hinckley.
⁶President Gordon B. Hinckley.
⁷First Presidency letter dated 15 September 1999.
⁸Dallin H. Oaks, "Gospel Teaching." *Ensign*, November 1999, p. 79.
⁹D. Cecil Clark. *Improving Your Church Teaching.* Provo, Utah: Community Press, 1983.

D. Cecil Clark. *Teaching Like the Master.* Provo, Utah: Covenant Communications, Inc., 1994.

CHAPTER 1

FUNDAMENTALS OF TEACHING EXPRESSED THROUGH CHURCH MATERIALS

An Overview

Education has long been a hallmark of the Church of Jesus Christ of Latter-Day Saints. Quality teaching and, more recently, teacher development have grown naturally from this emphasis. How has teacher development changed over the years? Early on, there was heavy and almost exclusive attention to technical skill development. In 1950, for example, an early pre–service training program titled Teaching the Gospel was developed for Sunday School teachers by Asahel D. Woodruff. In addition, he prepared a course supplement text titled *Teaching the Gospel*. We catch a flavor of the early philosophy about Church teaching from an interesting statement appearing in Chapter 21 of his book under a section titled "The Plan is a Map":

> A good lesson map has two main parts, a destination and a route. The destination is the objective. It should be an explicit statement of just what you want the class to have when the period ends. Don't confuse it with the statement of what you are going to do, or the material you are going to read, or the activities you are going to use. These are the means for reaching the objective. Means without a predetermined end will take us nowhere. The route is how you will reach the destination. It should be a concise and complete set of actions you intend the class members to engage in, and the ways in which you get them to do them. (p.163).

In an appendix of that manual, sample lessons are given, for example, "The Kingdom Finds Itself in the Presence of Evil." Notice the high degree of structure and detail in this lesson format:

1. Read in class the Parable of the Tares (Matthew 13:24-30).
2. Discuss such questions as "What is the danger of separating wheat and tares by some drastic means?" "How can preservation of every bit of good be a means of helping to eliminate evil?"
3. Have a few modern situations which illustrate this point, and be prepared to present them vividly.
4. Have a clear summary of the concept ready to use at the end of the discussion.

Clearly this early focus was on developing teaching techniques, "how to" approaches for teachers, by leading them through every step of the lesson.

As time has passed, more attention has been given to the teacher's personal development as well as technique development. President Packer's early and long-lived book *Teach Ye Diligently* represents a combination of teaching skills and teacher qualities. *Teaching, No Greater Call*, a periodically revised source book, gives attention to the teacher's personal qualities:

> What power do loving, caring, devotion to duty, selflessness, scripture study, fasting, and prayer give our teaching? Techniques and methods alone do not make us good teachers. This book has been prepared to assist you in both the spirit and the techniques of your calling as a teacher. . . . [It] is a resource book treating many topics that can help you improve both the spiritual and technical aspects of your gospel teaching. (p.iii)

In 1994, the *Teaching Guidebook* appeared:

> This guidebook discusses the example of the master teacher, Jesus Christ, and presents ways in which teachers can prepare themselves spiritually for their responsibilities. It explains how to organize a lesson and presents a variety of teaching methods that will help teachers make lessons interesting and effective. (p. iv)

In 1998, *Gospel Teaching and Leadership,* appeared in the *Church Handbook of Instructions.* The same pattern exists. For teacher characteristics, the handbook suggests such topics as "Seek the Spirit While Preparing a Lesson", "Be Humble", "Be Dedicated", and "Love Class Members". On the techniques side, there are sections such as "Use a Variety of Teaching Methods", "Help Class Members Apply What is Taught", and "Encourage Class Members to Participate". (p.iii)

Over time, then, greater attention has been given to the teacher's personal qualities. Other trends can be observed: movement toward simplification; emphasis on tailoring lessons to meet student needs; and flexibility to allow for inspiration. Teachers are encouraged to "make applications at the end of the lesson" in their own ways and through their own ideas. Modeling and sharing of ideas among teachers implies that a variety of techniques can be effectively employed. In lesson manuals, the old lists of painfully specific objectives have been replaced with fewer and more sensible objectives; there is greater acknowledgment that students may come away with different outcomes and different meanings from the lesson. Note this example from the *Church Handbook of Instruction*:

> Most Church manuals suggest questions to use. Teachers should seek guidance from the Spirit in deciding which questions to ask, how to organize them, how to ask them, and how to add to them. [1]

With good reason, the authors of our modern teacher development program assume a relationship between the personal characteristics of the teacher and the techniques he or she employs: Good people are better teachers. In this book, I will show *how* a teacher's goodness is reflected in his or her teaching and how that goodness makes a difference to the students *as the teacher teaches*. This relationship between goodness and technique, between personness of the teacher and methods used, will prove to be an important concept in the current book. We will see that the two are inextricably woven together, and they cannot be separated. Indeed, the method is an outward portrayal of the teacher's personhood.

Based on talks by our leaders and the wide range of teacher development materials produced by the Church, here are familiar fundamentals of good teaching:

1. Make prayerful and diligent preparation.
2. Study the scriptures continually.
3. Teach with the Spirit.
4. Be humble.
5. Love those whom you teach.
6. Focus on the students, their needs and their testimonies.
7. Be pure and live the gospel.
8. Teach the doctrine of Christ from prescribed manuals and the scriptures.
9. Use effective techniques (e.g. variety in methods, visual aids, questions, involvement of class members through discussions, inclusion of relevant stories and object lessons, attention to eye contact, adaptation of lessons to situations of class members).

Every teacher can bear testimony to the truthfulness and power of these fundamentals. The challenge is to *translate* them into your own life and your own teaching context and to maximize their effectiveness within that context.

---

[1]*Church Handbook of Instructions, Book 2, Section 16*, p. 33.

CHAPTER 2

THE INNER SELF

We Have A Spiritual Endowment

Our approach to teacher *development* is anchored in the knowledge that we are offspring of God and have inherited His divine nature: "Ye are gods; and all of you are children of the most high."[1] We are, therefore, moral beings endowed with intentions towards goodness: predispositions to respond in sympathy, support, help and caring to the daily obligations that confront us. This innate goodness can be developed through righteous choices or mired down by yielding to the promptings of Satan.

The "inner self" consists of our values, beliefs, character, personality, biography—our core, who we are. Through the Gospel we understand that this inner self is spiritual and, in addition to these other characteristics, possesses those that come with being an offspring of God.

Opposition in All Things—We Have Natural—Man Tendencies

King Benjamin, discussing the atonement of Christ, contrasts child and adult. We read: "For behold he judgeth, and his judgement is just; and the *infant* perisheth not that dieth in his infancy; but *men* drink damnation to their own souls except they humble themselves and become as little children" (italics added).[2] Though born with a divine nature—with a predisposition toward goodness—we come into a world of sin, and through our experiences "sin conceiveth in [our] hearts."[3] Then:

> For the natural man is an enemy to God, and has been from the fall of Adam, and will be, forever and ever, unless he yields to the enticings of the Holy Spirit, and putteth off the natural man and becometh a saint through the atonement of Christ the Lord, and becometh as a child, submis-

sive, meek, humble, patient, full of love, willing to submit in all things which the Lord seeth fit to inflict upon him, even as a child doth submit to his father."[4]

In their commentary on the *Book of Mormon*, McConkie and Millet explain, "To the extent that we resist the enticings of the Spirit we are at odds with God and in a state of rebellion against that which is divine within us."[5] As we grow and succumb to the temptations of evil we *become* carnal and end up in varying degrees a natural man or woman. This inner self, then, is subject to the temptations of Satan and to the scales of the natural man. In John we read, "They are of the world: therefore speak they of the world, and the world heareth them."[6]

Teaching is an Expression of The Inner Self

We are now ready to observe the influence of the inner self on our teaching. Let us consider several examples.

Case 1

My wife Gaile and I were returning to Provo after a visit with my mother, who was living in Denver, and we were facing the 100 mile desert stretch between Grand Junction, Colorado and Green River, Utah. We have witnessed its beauty many times, and this day I felt like a time-passing discussion would hurry our crossing. Since the quiet expanse beckons one back to the basics of life, I set forth a ponderous question based on our 39 years of marriage: "Gaile, how would you describe our marriage and me as your husband?" She grew silent for some moments. Following a number of warming comments about our marriage and our life as a couple, she turned to me as her husband. I had made respectable progress over the years; in many ways I was outstanding. Then came her startling observation, offered in a compassionate, matter-of-fact voice:

"You also have some anger inside—maybe because, as you have indicated to me in the past, you see yourself as less successful than you had always dreamed of being."

"You jest! I admit to some disappointment that my castles have been reduced to log cabins—but I'm certainly not angry about it."

"On one or two occasions while you were teaching, I've heard you tell the story of Elder Marvin J. Ashton's visit to a stake conference in California. In introducing Elder Ashton, the stake president reassuringly told of his own family—sons having gone on missions and all children marrying in the temple. Once at the pulpit, Elder Ashton turned to the stake president in a teaching moment said, 'President, you go home and kneel down in your closet and express thanks to your Heavenly Father, **but don't burden the rest of us with your successes!**' There has been excessive anger in your voice as you quoted that phrase. I've seen members of the audience startled by your intensity. Elder Ashton was a gentle, kindly, soft-spoken apostle. He never would have embarrassed that stake president or punished him with that tone of voice."

Suddenly the desert seemed vast, and there was no place to hide. It is in silence that truth finds you. I had not acknowledged these feelings, even to myself. But those I had taught had felt them.

<u>Case 2</u>

While serving as a bishop I had been counseling a warring couple who were intent upon destroying their marriage through mutual selfishness. There was no love between them, and there were irreconcilable conflicts in values. Each inflicted pain on the other, always strategic, always claiming to be the victim. Tears of discouragement and sadness flowed on both sides. Before the conflict had reached unsolvable proportions, I had called the husband to teach a class of 15-16 year-olds, which he dearly loved. Each Sunday he came fortified with optimism and stood hopefully before the class. One day I was approached by a young girl: "We like Brother B., but he seems sad. Sometimes he cries in class when there is nothing to cry about. Is he unhappy?"

This inner self, inclined toward goodness, still grappled with carnality and displayed it in teaching. Parker Palmer well expresses the struggle: "As I teach I project the condition of my soul onto my students, my subject, and our way of being together. The entanglements I experience in the classroom are often no more or less than the convolutions of my inner life."[7] In teaching we cannot hide our inner selves, nor should we, for, as Palmer states, this inner self "is the soil from which good teaching comes." *We teach who we are.*

Students in my classes at the university are planning careers as teachers in junior and senior high schools. Most are in the process of discovering their inner selves and exploring who they are as teachers. Here is a sample from their journals. Reflect on how this person's inner self would be projected in her classroom:

> "I see myself as being socially inept, insensitive, and unfeeling. I see myself as being intelligent, but I have an extremely difficult time expressing my thoughts or feelings verbally. I see myself as being tired, boring, and bored. I see myself always alone and unloved. I see myself as awkward, delicate, and afraid."

In contrast, what might be predicted from the next student's self description:

> "As a teacher . . . I first must establish my control of the situation and my 'dominance' over them [my students] before I can be persuaded to give some of this control back to them . . . . Once I feel that the students respect me and listen to what I say, then I will be willing to give them more freedom and let myself be more friendly and at ease with them. I hope that they will still feel that I care about them and be willing to come to me with problems or questions, but I know that I must establish myself as a teacher not to be messed with first, especially a new teacher."

Here is a student who realizes the influence of her inner self:

> "It's hard to hide what is really in your heart. When you are up in front of people for that long, you start to show yourself to your students whether you want to or not . . . . I have also discovered that when I am struggling with something, my teaching suffers in many ways. For instance, when I go to teach and there is an unresolved issue with one of my roommates, I am definitely not as effective. I find that I become distracted as I am preparing my lesson. My dedication and efforts are thwarted by feelings of uneasiness. It's harder to listen to the Spirit when there are issues

clouding my mind and heart. I also don't feel as connected to my students because I am so focused on myself."

Case 3

Kayo, father of three, is one of two elders quorum instructors. Work-related travel pulls him out of town too much for the good of his young family. Because he is often exhausted when he arrives home, personal recuperation rather than family involvement has become his pattern. Solo activities such as golf and running, though personally renewing, hardly provide relief for an overworked wife tied to three children. Couple time is often a tense tug-of-war between his work commitments and her family needs.

Attempting to leave his unresolved stress at the classroom door, Kayo slips on his performance hat and moves optimistically through this Sunday's lesson titled "Importance of Family." We all do this! We attempt to hide inner-self struggles in order to perform at our best on the Lord's errand. We salute ourselves for righteous desires and personal best efforts.

Though heroic, attempts to hide the inner self are impossible, especially over time. Well meaning, we have come to believe we can separate the inner self from our teaching, a convenient dualism. But this is a false project. *Teaching is an expression of the inner self.* Try as he might, Kayo cannot step out of his struggle with guilt during a lesson on the importance of families.

Visualize Kayo's classroom on this particular Sunday:

"I may not be the one to teach this lesson today, but I'll do my best." He is tense and guarded with this lesson—more so than usual- and finds safety in mechanically reading each scripture and telling both stories given in the manual. He asks a class member to stand and read marked sections of the Proclamation on the Family, and he is visibly uncomfortable as he senses the prophet is speaking directly to him. There is a lack of conviction in his presence, bordering on timidity. Asked to comment on Kayo's demeanor, a class member would likely say, "He's not comfortable up there—he's struggling inside with something." During the lesson, two elders comment on family practices they have adopted to promote greater cohesion among their family members. At the end of each comment Kayo thanks the brother and moves on with the lesson, not wanting to explore or generate further discussion. But another class member interrupts with disappointment: "That's not my family. I've got flexibility in my work, but my wife still complains I'm not home enough. I need your formula." Kayo acknowledges this brother's dilemma—too close for comfort—and hurries on.

Kayo's guardedness—his unwillingness to open up and honestly explore this issue—*is* the voice of his inner self. He might just as well have acknowledged at the beginning: "Brethren, here is my situation. I feel guilty about being selfish, about coming home and going off to play golf leaving my wife and children. Currently golf is my only form of self-renewal, and I have to have that to be a reasonably decent husband and father. You will undoubtedly detect this as I present this lesson on the importance of the family." Obviously, he could have used his own struggle as an effective beginning, since others were experiencing similar conflicts.

Case 4

Consider Chris, a mother of five who teaches Gospel Doctrine. Her hard-working husband manages a successful brokerage firm which, during its growth, consumed years of his time and energy. However, the rewards of his commitment are now being realized: large home, exotic trips, bonuses, prestige, and ample material benefits for his family. Over the years Chris has had to compete with the business for her husband's life, habitually coming out on the short end. A smoldering resentment has grown within her heart, unextinguished by travel, a new car, and lavish home furnishings.

No amount of preparatory makeup covers her internal enmity. Her heart becomes transparent through her teaching, often in subtle ways. While covering First Nephi, for example, she laments Sariah's subservient role to Lehi and points out Sariah's fortitude as Lehi's saving grace on more than one occasion. She identifies the importance of women in the lives of other men: Nephi, Laman and Lemuel, David, Joseph Smith. As comments arise about role differences between men and women, she presses for equality. When male-dominant comments arise in class, she returns to the theme running throughout her teaching: Brethren, give time and energy to your wives. They are an important part of your lives.

Case 5

Finally, consider Eric, a Gospel Essentials teacher who considers himself eminently successful and a bit superior to other people. Each personal experience shared during a lesson portrays him as having made the right decision, doing the right thing:

> "When I was mission president I told my missionaries . . . ." "In my successful business I always told my clients . . . ." "I may not always do the right thing, but whenever I find myself in this situation I . . . ." "When I served as branch president in the MTC, my missionary districts were always at the top of the . . . ." "I have never had a person come back to me and tell me that . . . ." At the same time, Eric sprinkles his lessons with playful self-deflating comments like "Correct me if I'm wrong . . . ." "You all know much more than I do about this . . . ." "I'm not the one to be teaching this class . . . . " "I'm not the greatest authority in the world but . . . ."

Eric's inner-self struggle goes something like this: I need to stress what I've done because I'm not confident with who I am.

We Purify The Inner Self Through Repentance

The inner self can undergo change, and these changes have important implications for others. "The angel's words 'becometh a saint' stresses that sanctification—becoming a saint—is indeed the labor of a lifetime, a process rather than a singular spiritual experience or event."[8] The life-long shedding of the natural man—daily repentance—opens the way for work toward Christ-centered lives ("forsaketh" *and* "cometh"[9]). The very shedding itself is movement toward goodness, towards the sanctified individual. When selfishness is given up, what is left? Our innate goodness. *Peeling off layers of the natural man leaves the inner self with its goodness.*

The scales with which we cover our inner selves can be many and varied: selfishness, pride, jealously, resentment, enmity, guilt, duplicity, fraudulence, self-promotion, strategy, manipulation, defensiveness, impatience, hardness of heart, jealousy, and resentfulness. Here are samples of people who are preparing to be teachers, as they shed some of these scales—setting their inner selves on a course towards goodness:

> "Though I am unsure of myself, I am in the process of becoming known to myself and allowing my personal truths to emerge. I feel like it's spring when the whole world begins to break forth and new life begins to grow. It's the most invigorating and freeing feeling!"

> "I think I am becoming less selfish. Before it was always 'How can I change this person to understand *my* point of view?' Now I say, 'How can I change myself to understand what this person's point of view is and, in turn, how can I change my attitude or feelings to resolve this meaningless conflict?"

As The Inner Self is Purified, a Person's Teaching Changes in Student-benefitting Ways

Here is one teacher's insight into how her inner change will benefit her students:

> "At times, it has been hard to make the connection between the changes I have made as a person and how these changes relate to the way I teach. The person I am and the teacher I am are the same. . . . All I was doing was just adding more layers of the natural man instead of peeling them off and letting my true self show forth. All the changes that have been made to me the person have also been made to me the teacher. . . . Since I am less manipulative as a person, I am less manipulative as a teacher. Since I am more compassionate as a person, I am more compassionate as a teacher, and so on."

We begin to more clearly understand Palmer's statement that the inner self is the "soil from which good teaching comes." It is also the soil from which tangled teaching comes, as we have witnessed in the five foregoing cases: my anger, the unloving husband's sadness, Kayo's selfishness, Chris' resentment, and Eric's pride. *Most of us are good teachers struggling with natural man tendencies on our way to becoming excellent teachers.* Goodness is a powerful human trait, and persons who have it draw us to them. I have observed changes in teacher's teaching as their goodness grows, changes which directly benefit their students. Following are some changes that occur and their effect upon our students.

An Awakening

Elder Marion D. Hanks was addressing a group of saints as he returned from an extended Church assignment. Said he, "Before I left I knew the Gospel was true—now I *really* know the Gospel is true."

A brother who with his wife had recently been released from missionary service in a third-world country soberly announced during his report, "I have always appreciated my life in Provo and have never taken for granted the blessings of living here. After our labors this past 18 months I *really* appreciate living in this valley."

A sister missionary, bearing testimony for the first time during a zone conference, testified that she knew the Lord had called her to serve and that her testimony of the work was strong. At her last zone conference, she again offered her testimony: "All my life I have known the Gospel is true, and today I know more surely than ever before." Experiences have a way of deepening what we already know, *awakening in us* more sure realizations. Repentance has the same effect: It melts us down, removes the darkness from our eyes, allows us to see more clearly and to learn more intensely what we already know. Indeed, *repentance is learning.*

Repentance and time spent with a class bring this same awakening: a deeply ingrained realization that what we are doing with these students is *truly* important and that we have an intense responsibility. Imagine an extreme case. Branden has been called to teach an adult class of which he is one of the youngest members. In the midst of law school, initially educated as an historian, he feels reasonably capable of standing in front of the group and talking about the New Testament. Early on, he regularly invokes light sarcasm and a quick wit as he moves in and out of scriptural passages, addressing events and principles with flippant questions. His cutesy approach draws attention to himself; he enjoys teaching with a flair. Months pass, and Branden settles into his teaching. A discomfort grows within. Something is wrong. Prayer and struggle and repentance ensue. A piercing realization: "What am I doing? These good, humble people come to class respecting my calling as teacher, expecting to be taught the saving truths of the Gospel. What meets them? A circus master!"

I have paraphrased a sample of comments from journals kept by students undergoing this awakening:

> "Teaching is serious business, far more so than I had ever imagined!"

> "I'm a steward over lives for this moment in time. I have power in me to help or hinder their progress toward salvation—and I will be held accountable for my teaching."

> "Since I have been called to teach this class, I must be the best the Lord has at this moment. He has placed responsibility on none other."

> "Only now am I coming to realize how cavalier I've taken my calling, how little preparation and commitment I've shown."

> "I've taken this calling seriously from day one; but I'm beginning to see just how serious it really is."

> "I have been evading my responsibility to be the best teacher that is in me to be. Time to roll up my sleeves and start affecting lives."

> "I've been blaming the kids, their parents, the room, the poor lesson manuals. Time to stop and start doing what I've been called to do."

What effect does this awakening have on students? Visionize the possibilities through your own life. Two immediately surface: students receive powerful spiritual food through your deeper preparation, and they are willing to partake of it because of the respect you show them.

Growing Authenticity

I was conducting an evaluation in a high school, which included interviewing a sample of students about the teaching that was occurring in their classrooms. In one small-group interview I asked a question about the discussions their teacher conducted. Bolting from the question, one student blurted out, "The whole problem with Mr. J. is that he's counterfeit!" Another jumped in, "Yeah, he's just not who he really is." Another offered a mellower description, "If he'd just stop pretending, kids would like him better. Why can't he just be himself and let us all deal with that?" Another set forth an explanation, "Everyone knows he's unsure of himself and that's why he tries to act so knowledgeable. He's so busy trying to be this great biologist he can't concentrate on us."

Repenting thaws out our inner selves, melting away pretensions, posturing, duplicity, and all other falseness we choose to construct. Teachers may attempt to "put on my teaching personality" in order to cover a snarled or broken inner self, and most attempt it with the best of intentions:

> "These kids should not have to be subjected to the struggles I'm having with my own daughter who is their age."

> "I just think you should always put your best foot forward—moving ever on regardless of the person you may be at that point in time."

> "Plain and simple. I want my students to believe I understand the scriptures and that I know more than they do—to warrant their respect and my calling as their teacher."

> "I'm just trying to survive! I don't want them to know how terrified I am each week and how hard this is for me. I try to put on a front so they won't see my fear."

We all salute the teacher who, regardless of personal struggle, goes before class each Sunday with hopes of building testimonies. All of us have experienced this and have felt the Spirit's buoying influence to carry us through. Credit students for being able to see into the souls of their teachers. Mr. J., the high school teacher, evokes a quite different set of reactions than would the teachers quoted above. His "counterfeit" nature is self-promoting, designed to enhance his own image. On the other hand, the four quoted teachers are putting on a good front for their students, not themselves, attempting to be *other* rather than *self-centered*. Repentance produces greater authenticity which, in turn, positively affects students. Note these comments by aspiring teachers coming to grips with their struggle to be authentic:

> "I need to open myself up to my students (and to myself)."

> "I'm becoming more who I really am rather than presenting a false self."

> "My life needs to become more of my message."

> "I have learned to focus less on what students feel about me, and more on what they feel about the subject."

> "I realized that maybe the reason why I worried about my students liking me is the fact that I am not really secure about who I am."

> "I am a little more authentic and this has carried over into my teaching. My teaching is more personal. I give more opinions and personal examples in my teaching. I am more relaxed and less concerned about a glossy presentation."

> "Through learning how to be more myself when I teach, I have learned how to calm my nerves and have gained more confidence. This in turn helps me perform at a higher level than before . . . . Through being honest with myself, I will have an easier time being honest with my students."

> "Another way I have overcome the barrier between me and the student is by being more open, or in other words, less deceiving, less manipulating, and less justifying . . . . I used to model and deceive, trying to appear more knowledgeable than I really was. Now I have no reservation to saying, 'I don't know.' My students appreciate my honesty and accept my answers more readily."

"There is less desire in my life now to seek after external acceptance, to worry about how I am perceived . . . . I must sacrifice my fear, pride, etc. by letting myself be vulnerable."

"Before, I was afraid of opening myself up; now I realize how crucial it is."

For these teachers, a natural result of repentance is greater genuineness, being the person you really are and valuing it—in front of your students.

For the first time, we catch a glimpse of how seeing teaching as an expression of the inner self can guide our thinking. We are given the following admonition: "Use a variety of methods in your teaching (e.g. lecture, group discussion, object lessons, games)." Is it really variety in our methods we need to be after—or is it something else? Here is an alternative suggestion: *Select and improve personal methods which permit your inner self the greatest access to your students–since the inner self makes the greatest difference.* Immediately the anxiety-prompted question arises: But what if my inner self is so embryonic, barren or forlorn that it detracts from rather than builds testimonies? The answer lies within each of us.

How does growing authenticity benefit students? Again, unnumbered possibilities arise. Here are two: students themselves become more authentic and are thereby compelled to shoulder their responsibility to learn and grow; and mutual respectful grows, which opens the way for students to bond with the teacher and the subject.

Greater Offering of Self

Authenticity is being real; offering of self adds the dimension of being other-centered, selfless. Once following an Education Week lecture I was approached by an elder's quorum president. He lamented that he had difficulty in getting quorum members to teach the group. When he had approached one well-educated and perfectly competent class member with a request to teach next week's lesson, he had received the answer, "No, I can't. I would be willing to teach in the Relief Society, or the youth—but there is too much testosterone in our group!" This elder felt he would be thrown into the lions' den and "eaten alive."

To make an offering of the self, the teacher asks, "What is required of me?" This is very different from the common response, "Why won't they pay attention to my lesson?" The other-centered teacher asks at lesson's end, "Did I bless lives today?" while the regular teacher asks, "How well did I do in presenting my lesson?" What does the selfless teacher offer to his or her students? Everything! Whatever it takes. You may be required to sacrifice your pride, your favorite sins, your time, your comfort, your control, your expertise, your long-held orientations, even your favorite methods, responses, stories, jokes—whatever sacrifice is necessary to bless lives of students on a particular day in a particular lesson.

Perhaps few teachers are ready for this level of selflessness with their students; nonetheless we can visualize its effect and at least make progress in that direction. Here are comments by young teachers struggling to offer more of themselves:

"I'm holding back less, offering my whole self to students."

"I have been more aware of teachers who aren't afraid or ashamed to dig deep into parts of their handbags to help benefit others. Teachers like this do not try to display certain features of their packages while covering others, but allow their suitcases to be accessible for their students to freely rummage through and take what is useful.

"I am offering students my emotional safety, one of my dearest possessions."

"My agenda is becoming less diluted—I'm getting beyond my needs for recognition and applause and having no other purpose but to bless lives."

"When I spend time and energy trying to impress my students, I am cheating them by splitting my attention between their needs and my self-image. This is a humbling insight."

"I forgot to reach out to others. I was so concerned with how I was doing that I turned away from others. . . . Serving is what teaching is all about, and I should have increased my serving ability.

"The greater my expertise, the more I can sacrifice it to my students."

Habitual impediments keep us stumbling toward this level of other-centeredness: fear, pride, need for emotional safety, incompetence, vulnerabilities, thirst for success. Such impediments impact our ways of thinking about teacher/student relationships. As our ability to sacrifice grows, we let go of self-interest, self-promotion, recognition—the fulfillment of self—for the needs and development of our students. Father Lehi showed this level of other centeredness in his feelings towards his sons: "And I have none other object save it be the everlasting welfare of your souls."[10] It is only deeper repentance that gradually frees us to shift focus from self to others.

Benefits to student from a self-sacrificing teacher are obvious. This disposition to concentrate on the needs of your students causes you to tailor your lessons, which creates greater interest and relevance for your students. Further, they feel your offering and respond with a willingness to take seriously your insights and testimony—and your assignments.

Growing Respect

Time and again while I am interviewing teenagers, two traits emerge as they describe their very best teachers: "He cares for us," and "She respects us." At the other end, pride—that subtle form of selfishness—is pervasive among the teachers who do not reach these young people. It must be the preferred characteristic of the natural man. As pride is surrendered through repentance, humility and respect take its place. Students can hardly resist a teacher who listens carefully to their comments and shows the courtesy of offering an honest response. Perhaps it is *inadvertent* disrespect that is frequently observed among Church teachers. In marching through their lessons, some teachers fail to see how certain types of comments and mannerisms communicate to students that their voices are not important: The teacher who looks at his watch or turns to her notes while a student is sharing a personal episode; the teacher who finishes sentences for students; the teacher who, with a quick "Thank you," moves briskly from one comment to the next; the teacher who is thinking up a retort while waiting for a student to finish her comment.

Respectful teachers promote respect in their students. If every student comment and question is respected, the quality improves, and students become teachable; they feel valued for having come to class, for struggling with personal testimony, for their desire to learn. This mutual respect opens the learning space for students; they feel safe in a respectful setting. Following is a sample of paraphrased comments by young new teachers:

> "I now realize and accept that students have absolute veto power over their own learning."

> "I have stopped lovingly bending their agency through manipulation—the ends never justify the means in teaching the Gospel."

> "I stopped trying to manipulate people . . . . After I realized that my actions in that regard were all self-promoting . . . . I started to focus more on service and submissiveness . . . . I tried to learn more about myself so that I could be a better friend to those I loved."

> "I'm willing to give up my power and control over you." [11]

> "I've stopped insisting on the rightness of my message and have stopped insisting they learn it."

> "The best thing a teacher can do to earn students' respect is to not worry about earning students' respect and to simply worry about teaching them the subject matter."

> "I, and I'm sure that many other students as well, have had to deal with teachers who patronize. I believe that this is one of the most harmful things that a teacher can do to a student. It can take away their confidence and self-esteem, and it makes going to the class a difficult experience. And I don't think that teachers do it because they wish to be mean. I think that it reveals what is going on in the teacher's mind and how he/she is thinking about their students. . . . Teachers patronize students because somewhere inside they believe that they are better than their students because they are more

experienced and knowledgeable or because they feel threatened by their students and they need to somehow put themselves above them."

<u>Growing Compassion</u>

While not an inevitable consequence of repentance, compassion can take root and flourish when repentance occurs. Of all the evidences of growing in goodness, compassion is the most powerful.

One day in a Gospel Doctrine class the teacher was plumbing the Parable of the Prodigal Son. A class member volunteered, "We are the older brother who sees his younger brother as undeserving of the father's coat." Silence fell over the room for a few moments while that comment was being processed. Then a sister quietly countered, "No, we are all the prodigal son."

While I was serving as a bishop, the highlight of my Sunday was sitting at the front of Primary during opening exercises. I loved to watch the guileless and fully transparent little faces which announce every feeling and response. Without even identifying the adult who was telling the story or leading the song, I could always tell how much that adult loved the children by looking into their faces. Children are gathered in by adults who love them, unable to resist their presence. By contrast, children can also feel when love is withheld by their teachers. They squirm, lose contact, talk, and shy away.

Only more subtle, we adults are like children in our need to be loved. Not even the oldest saint, patiently enduring on the back row, leafing through tattered scriptures, can insulate him or herself from a loving younger teacher. Regardless of experience or scholarly differences, the elder member cannot help but respond to love from this shiny new teacher, painfully less informed on Gospel subjects.

Cheri teaches Relief Society in a BYU ward, an intimidating experience since all the girls are at least her age, and half are older and more experienced. She does all the right things: fasts for help, prays with fervor and devotion, importunes the Spirit for guidance, gives elegant lessons, responds thoughtfully to comments and questions, involves the girls and bears strong testimony. One Sunday night after chocolate cake, Cheri asks Stacy, her ever supportive roommate, to assess her teaching.

"You're a great teacher—the girls have told you that."

"I am aware of what some girls have told me after a lesson—but what is your impression?"

"All your wonderful talent and gifts go into your teaching, but one thing is missing—you don't love them."

"Should I? I mean I certainly care for them; I'm interested in their welfare. I show my caring by my preparation. But I mean these are college-age women. They want the Gospel understanding, not my love. Leave that to the boys not to their Relief Society teacher."

Of all characteristics a teacher can possess—at any age level—the ability to love students is the most critical. Countless stories can be told of a loving teacher who has turned a life around. Years later, college students being interviewed will say, "I don't remember what she taught us, but I can remember how she loved us." Gospel scholarship and preparation are never substitutes for love among good teachers. Rather, their teaching vibrates with it.

Here are paraphrased statements of teachers acknowledging the role of love:

"Although my message is important, my love for them is more so."

"My growing love for students is not indulgent love—I am doing whatever will most bless their lives."

"I grieve for students rather than criticize them."

"No matter what a student says or does, I am no longer offended."

"I'm less concerned about getting through the material and more focused on what I can do to help my students."

"I'm allowing my love for students to compete with my fears about teaching them—I may not be making progress with my fears, but I am progressing in my love."

"I feel like my desire to love people more has also made me want to make positive changes in my teaching habits. I do not want to become a better teacher so that I can win awards and have a respectable name, but my desire stems from a wish to teach people as opposed to subjects and to love them as Christ loves them . . . . I do not want . . . to ignore questions and comments so I can get through with presenting the information."

Love from the teacher triggers love in return, which makes the message believable:

"Because he loves me, his message must be important—else why would he be presenting it to me?" Ample research tells us that when students value their teacher—care for him or her—their commitment and learning are enhanced. But there is an added advantage seldom mentioned: When students care for their teacher and are earnest about wanting to learn and grow, the teacher is inspired to heroic preparation and competence.

Growing Meekness and Submissiveness

Finally, we come to pride, the most tightly-held characteristic of the natural man. Because pride is the unparalleled deterrent to effective teaching, a detailed discussion is appropriate. Pride haunts us all, with its many subtle faces. Pride is masked selfishness, puffiness, exaggerated feelings of self-importance. It turns us selfishly inward; it blunts our innate goodness so we cannot hear others' voices, consider their situations, understand—or even care about—their needs. Pride keeps us from turning outward to others; we insulate ourselves from personal involvement with their lives. Pride defines the teaching role solely in terms of the teacher's performance. When students intrude on tightly-structured presentations, the teacher becomes impatient; when they question, the teacher becomes defensive, brittle, uncorrectable. Alma would have us right ourselves in our thinking: "For the preacher was no better than the hearer, neither was the teacher any better than the learner; and thus they were all equal."[12]

Tradition works against us. From the one-room schoolhouse in the early twentieth century comes the image of the all-knowing teacher informing unlearned students. This image hardly fits contemporary Church classrooms. Neither does the image of prideful pharisees, puffy and ostentatious, scornfully preaching to the poor, unwashed and illiterate. Pride in modern classrooms is subtle, cloaked in brittleness, defensiveness, light sarcasm, self-focus, self-promotion, impatience, manipulation, and inability to receive correction. So elusive is this sin—all dressed up—that teachers are often shocked to discover that their defensiveness, for example, is not fear at all, but pride. Or they may discover that their self-focus is not insecurity at all, but pride. Even further, could "insecurity" itself be a form of pride? (Is Kayo really unsure of himself?)

Pride is not to be confused with honest intention. Teachers frequently make comments like the following: "I have been called to teach by a Priesthood leader. It therefore becomes my responsibility to study and grow in Gospel knowledge until I *do know* more than my students—so I can lead them to correct principles." This attitude is not pride, but a righteous desire to fulfill a calling from the Lord.

We must be ever vigilant. Satan is superbly clever and sophisticated. He waits for a season. Our knowledge and expertise develops as does our success. Students offer sincere compliments and expressions of thanks: "That was a great lesson today," "You are a very good teacher," "I wish my grasp of the Gospel was like yours," "You certainly understand the scriptures," "I so enjoy your lessons," "I love to come to your class every Sunday," "I wish all teachers in the Church were like you," "Thank you, thank you." Time passes, and you accumulate a backlog of successful experiences—and accolades. (Time is so important in developing pride.) Then deceptively simple thoughts arise in your mind: "No question about it, you are a good teacher—you deserve the credit—notice how your students have come to respect you—*now* how do you see yourself?" The steps from successfully fulfilling one's calling, to self-validation, to the beginnings of pride are subtle indeed.

A personal example may be instructive. I started my teaching career as a shiny new assistant professor at the University of Washington: "Publish, teach well, make a name for yourself, develop a reputation, manage your career" were my governing values. (My own professors had taught me well.) Palmer cuts right to the source of my early motivation: "But we find it easier to seek facts that keep us in power than truths that require us to submit."[13] My teaching paradigm was clear: Stand at the podium delivering neatly-crafted lectures to underling students who obediently take notes later to be memorized and artfully delivered on examinations–the knower informing the unknowing. Not all was pomp and ceremony. I *was* committed to helping students learn and prepare to successfully function in their chosen vocations. Yet that early in my career I had no awakening of the kind mentioned in this chapter. Further, my authenticity, offering of self, respect, compassion, and meekness were rudimentary, sporadic and, sadly, sometimes fabricated. I shall never forget the icon students one day posted on my office door. It was a cartoon of a lion sitting in a cage with tail drooping out through the bars. A brave young boy was pictured yanking the tail with a mocking chuckle while the surprised lion looked on. The scribbled-in caption read, "Take that Dr. Clark!" My naivete and utter insulation were revealed when I became amused rather than sobered by the message.

Years passed, many of them. Two years ago I wrote a short article which permits a comparison between my early and later teaching career. As I re-read it, I can see progress in my own struggle with pride—and some growth. I share it in the spirit of instruction.

A wise chief remarked, "It is in the darkness of their eyes that men lose their way—not the darkness of the path." I was bred into and have been nurtured by the professorial teaching model. For me this model has been the Mosaic law of academea to which I have faithfully—and lovingly—adhered for some 28 years. There is about it strictness, structure, specificity, and certainly safety. Roles are defined. I am the teacher, the expert. Benevolently paternalistic, I feel qualified to decide what is best for the students to learn and how it should be learned. Students, though well intentioned, need structure, direction, control, motivation. My responsibility is to do things *to* the students in order to extract the learning I have chosen for them. Failure results from not invoking the right strategy or technique. Clearly defined requirements, assignments, readings, note-taking procedures, in addition to well crafted and discriminating tests, clear cut-off points for grades, punctuality and attendance—happily, the students can't miss. We are safe and comfortable knowing what is expected of each other. Neither seriously disrupts the other's role. The students are students and I am the professor, one who dispenses thoughtfully-packaged knowledge along with some wisdom. Students come into my classes to learn my truths, hard earned through years of personal study. Fortunately, some want my knowledge.

Classroom life is occasionally grumpy, more often respectful and courteous as we dutifully play out our roles. At semester's end I conclude, "I did my part; I was there, ready, prepared. I think they learned—at least those who were serious about learning."

Now, in my twilight years, I have found the courage to think beyond this faithful role, my friend which has established me as "professor" over the years. Perhaps it is meltdown. Perhaps it is the chronic suspicion that if students came into my classes to earnestly learn their own truths, even my poorest teaching would satisfy their need. An exacting look reveals that my structured and formalized requirements have more often than not invited students to evade their obligation to learn. Indeed, the greater my control, the more superficial their commitment. The more I motivate, the less motivated they become. The more strictly I define roles, the more we remain strangers. The more elegant my lectures, the more sporadic the attendance. (I seem to have a form of godliness but deny the power thereof.)

I propose an alternative role: the submissive professor, one who submits freely to his obligation to the students. Rather than "How do I get students to take responsibility?" I ask, "What is required of me?" I come to meet the students with everything I have, ready to improvise, to depart from the prescribed curriculum, even to relinquish my own framework if necessary at a given moment. As the teacher I am transformed through the act of teaching. Professional distance dissolves in my vulnerability before my students. My success depends on them. I am responding rather than resisting the obligation to respond. This coming to the students with my all, including my vulnerability, awakens the students' obligation to me, and through me to what I teach. The students also can choose to accept or to resist this ever-present obligation. Witnessing the fulfillment of my obligation, the students more often reach out to me—come to me—in fulfilling their obligation. Beside this internal "motivating" force, my early external attempts at motivation are pale. As teacher and taught, we experience mutual obligations as moral human beings. Teaching is a pervasively moral experience.

This act of submission, of humbling oneself before the students in awakening and fulfilling moral obligations, does not shatter the professorial model; rather, it goes beyond. Meekness and submission may become the highest form of teaching as they free up the most powerful variable of human interaction: fulfillment of mutual obligation. "... learn of me; for I am meek and lowly in heart...." (Matthew 11:29).

So, I ask myself, is my road to improved teaching marked by repentance, stripping away academic pride, humbly going before my students? As my heart changes, do I change the way I apply my methods and the way my students receive what I offer? Do I change the way I lecture, interact with students, handle questions, establish course requirements, make assessments, grade my students' efforts? Yes, in my case.

I continue to seek new teaching approaches, tips, techniques. My repertoire expands through experience, conversations, reading. But no longer do I routinely invoke my pre-determined strategies, activities, or even curricula. In a given moment, the Spirit may prompt me to improvise, depart, use an approach I have not anticipated—or prepared—as I quietly respond to the question I continually ask: "What is required of me?" When the moment is there, the event must be experienced, and the notes may not be taken.

How easy to assume that if a teacher becomes meek and submissive (to students and to the subject) the teacher-student relationship will break down: Teacher will lose credibility and effectiveness; students will no longer be students and havoc will ensue.

Following are statements of newly-developing teachers as they examined meekness in their own teaching:

> "I do not have to establish myself as a teacher. I worry less about power and control, about whether they see me as an authority."

> "My methods are used to serve, not to control or manipulate."

> "It is important for me to be transformed by the teaching experience; I will become a student with you, and we will both change."

> "I am fighting my tendency to speak too much to want to enlighten others ... shifting perspectives have a great impact in my actions .... In teaching I am trying to let myself be known to students instead of standing aside, afraid of my weaknesses or putting myself above to hide ... to love instead of posture ... bringing my actions up to my ideals through this peeling, repenting process."

We have already examined the benefits to students taught by submissive teachers: realization of their own responsibility to learn; tendency to give up their own pride and become submissive learners; greater freedom to explore and develop their own truths.

Relaxation and Serenity

Years ago, prior to the three-hour block of meetings, Primary-age children were asked to give 2 1/2 minute talks to the congregation during Sunday School opening exercises. These talks were often more traumatic for the parents than for the children, sometimes requiring extravagant preparation and rehearsal. Invariably, mothers sat on the second row, mouthing the words and ready with prompts in case of a memory lapse. When the performance was completed, a sigh of relief, followed by a quiet smile replaced the anxiety—on the face of the mother. While no mother (including my own) would admit it, the child's performance was seen as a direct reflection on the parents. Smoothly-presented stories within a memorized talk cast a brighter glow on the family than false starts by an unprepared child who was attempting to read the talk his mother had hurriedly written that morning. While we can understand such anxiety, the phenomenon reveals something about motives. When we are worried about how our students see us or when we are trying to impress them, large amounts of energy are unnecessarily expended over our heightened anxiety.

Through repentance we surrender our intentions to impress, and we concentrate on carrying out the Lord's will in our teaching. Freedom and relief come by giving up falseness, pretensions, posturing and internal dividedness.

Repentance reorients teachers' perspectives, helping them see their limitations in working with students. With the best of intentions we can become caught up and carried away, and then we revert to control and manipulation. Especially with teenagers, teachers are tempted to want to engineer their students' lives: "If I can prevent even one episode of sexual misconduct I'll try about anything." "If I can bring tears to their eyes from this video, they may think twice before trying drugs." "I used drama to hook the students, then I got them to promise they would never indulge." As teachers respect student agency, they tend to be more relaxed and serene in their teaching.

Note these comments by students and teachers:

"As I have learned how to be authentic and vulnerable, my teaching and relationships have progressed. I can accept others for their otherness and their differences, and I can make music with the variation in the people around me . . . . I am also better able to relax and to let others discover knowledge themselves. Rather than fearing to let go and feeling a need to force my relationship with a subject, students, or other people, I can let others be their own 'meaning-makers.' I am also better able to just let the subject or relationship move naturally and incubate in the silences . . . and my teaching has reached a different level."

"During this period, I have noticed that as my personality has mellowed, so has my teaching. I know this is due, in part, to my increasing comfort with not controlling every situation. As a teacher, I used to feel that I needed to have control over everything that happened. Along with this assumption came a lot of unnecessary responsibility and guilt."

Students are less intimidated and more open around a serene and unhurried teacher. Teachers are easier to believe, and students, even older ones, are reassured by the teacher's confidence. Most important, students feel the teacher is unencumbered with personal agendas and clear about the will of the Lord—and they are inclined to be also.

Growing Student Commitment

Imagine a less-than-mediocre high school teacher who, because of waning desire, disorganization, forgetfulness, outdated subject matter, and vacillation begins to lose students. They skip classes, show up late, argue about assignments, turn work in late, do poorly on exams, and sleep and talk to each other during his teaching. This regrettable teacher attempts to justify his behavior: "These irresponsible kids don't deserve my best efforts—they're lazy and unaccountable. They come expecting to be motivated and spoon fed." Now imagine, further, an abrupt change in the students. Each makes a full commitment to the class: consistent attendance, carefully completed assignments, thoughtful test performances, genuine interest and respect. This change has a sobering effect on the teacher: "Look at their commitment. These students have come to learn. I'm the one to teach them and there's work to do." The captives have freed the captor!

All along this instructor has experienced a moral obligation to be a good teacher, to help his students learn, to be the best he can be—this is his spiritual endowment. But he holds back, resists or flees from this obligation. He camouflages it even from himself under all the self-justifying excuses. *But the changes he witnesses in his students–their commitment to be good students—re-awakens his own commitment to be the best teacher he can be.* Their willingness melts away his excuses, leaving his moral obligation boldly before him. He can continue to resist his obligation, or he can follow it, but he cannot ignore it. Their commitment becomes his call to arms. The greater their growth, the greater his desire to improve. There is no end to the possibilities for his improvement.

A teacher can also turn to the Lord for help in facing this moral obligation. Here is a person's acknowledgment of this source:

> "As I develop my relationship with Him [the Savior] through obedience to His laws, I become ever more aware of His love for me, and of my ability—even my responsibility—to improve. I find motivation therein to begin the process to change. Perhaps more importantly, I find the essential patience needed to be gracious to myself in the midst of my inadequacies."

A Final Word

From this chapter we glimpse the inner self. If you could work on only one aspect of your teaching, one aspect that would make the greatest *single* difference in your teaching, it would be your inner self. Repentance brings about powerful results in your teaching. If you want to see a change in your teaching, try it.

We cannot stop here. Saints can be wonderful people but still be eminently forgettable as teachers. A right-hearted teacher, painfully inept in relating to students or in representing the subject, may be nearly as ineffective as a wrong-hearted teacher with the slickest of approaches. The voyage continues.

[1] Psalm 82:6.
[2] Mosiah 3:18.
[3] Moses 6:55; see also Romans 3:23; D & C 93:1.
[4] Mosiah 3:19.
[5] Joseph F. McConkie & Robert L. Millet. *Doctrinal Commentary on the Book of Mormon,* Volume II–Jacob through Mosiah, 1988, p. 152.
[6] 1 John 4:5.
[7] Parker J. Palmer. *The Courage To Teach.* San Francisco: Jossey-Bass, 1998, p.2.
[8] Joseph F. McConkie & Robert L. Millet. *Doctrinal Commentary on the Book of Mormon,* Volume II–Jacob through Mosiah, 1988, p.153.
[9] Doctrine and Covenants 93:1.
[10] 2 Nephi 2:30.
[11] See Doctrine and Covenants 121.
[12] Alma 1:26.
[13] Parker J. Palmer. *To Know As We Are Known*, San Francisco: Harper, 1983, p. 40.

CHAPTER 3

STUDYING YOUR TEACHING

Spent Hopes

Again, the mix of frustration and discouragement—and a twinge of anger. How hard can it be to get a lesson into the lives of five Laurels? They come, quietly polite, guarded, uninvolved. Once in a while I leave with good feelings about the way the lesson went, but much of the time it ends up flat. On one Sunday everything goes into the lesson: powerful message, relevant story, good questions (I thought), pictures, a video, background music. Another week, not nearly as prepared, I get the same results. Pulling out answers and drumming up short-lived discussions leaves me drained. Am I supposed to be working this hard presenting a lesson? I sometimes come away with hives. I'm friendly, I ask questions about their schoolwork and their social lives—I show interest in them. But repayment is distance, coolness. They seem to be saying, "You can't come in." But there are signs of a flourishing inner circle: silent note passing, a secretive whisper, eye signals across the room. This is maddening. So much is happening in their lives outside of parental influence and involvement in their activities. I can help them. Tamara, my rescuer, regularly volunteers answers to my questions, but I suspect she plays the role of supportive teenager without becoming involved in the lesson itself. I think she feels sorry for me. Laura is a time bomb waiting to explode. She is unlike either parent and bristles when compared to her straight-laced sister. She endures contemptuously, says nothing, and leaves. Megan, insecure and frivolous, busies herself with chewing gum, corralling her hair behind each ear, and pulling at her too-short skirts. She is always getting ready to get on task but never actually doing so. Nichole is obedient to a fault but afraid of her own shadow. Scriptures faithfully open, she sits motionless with a dutiful stare. I wonder what goes on inside that squeaky clean countenance? Tosha seems to be hurting inside, struggling with her testimony, her parents, or her boyfriend—or all of them.

But no one would ever know. It's like she is afraid of shocking the rest of us with her true feelings. Each girl has her own way of "sitting through class"—patient endurance.

Were I a novice, I would be less self-critical. But I've worked effectively with Beehives and mixed Sunday School classes. Adding to the irony, I took the Teaching The Gospel Course and honestly tried to apply what I already knew and had reinforced by the course: pray, prepare, teach with the Spirit, love those whom you teach. Three weeks ago, I invited Sister Thompson (the teacher improvement coordinator) in to observe. She complimented me on my well organized lessons, suggested more class discussion, and advised me to keep working to know the girls. She was supportive and tried to be helpful.

I'm investing a lot of prayer and effort, feeling discouraged, and realizing little success. What am I to do now? More preparation? Greater patience? ("It will come.") Or, heaven forbid, are my Laurels impossibly unreachable?

The familiar fundamentals of good teaching remain valid: Love those whom you teach, be an example, teach basic gospel truths, be set apart, pray often, study the scriptures, live the gospel, prepare spiritually, identify resources, begin preparing early, prepare to teach the main idea, study the supporting ideas, plan a summary and challenge, get to know class members, allow class members to participate, use stories and examples, use pictures and objects, use music, ask meaningful questions, invite special guests, bear testimony, pray with class members. Allyson, our Laurel teacher, reviewed these fundamentals while reading *Teaching, No Greater Call: A Resource Guide for Gospel Teaching,* reading assigned talks by the Brethren, and participating in the Teaching The Gospel Course. Given her teaching experience and her willingness to apply these principles, why would her success with the Laurels be less than she desired?

Calling On Her Own Resources

Discouraged but resolute, Allyson continues petitioning the Lord for help. The Lord has called her, He will bless her. But what about calling on her own resources? Can she assist the Spirit in answering her prayers, even expand opportunities for the Spirit to inspire her? Consider this apocryphal story:

> In the year of our Lord 1432, there arose a grievous quarrel among the brethren over the number of teeth in the mouth of a horse. For 13 days the disputation raged without ceasing. All the ancient books and chronicles were fetched out, and wonderful and ponderous erudition, such as was never before heard of in this region, was made manifest. At the beginning of the 14th day, a youthful friar of goodly bearing asked his learned superiors for permission to add a word, and straightway, to the wonderment of the disputants, whose deep wisdom he sore vexed, he beseeched them to unbend in a manner coarse and unheard-of, and to look in the open mouth of a horse and find an answer to their questionings. At this, their dignity being grievously hurt, they waxed exceedingly wroth; and, joining in mighty uproar, they flew upon him and smote him hip and thigh, and cast him out forthwith. For, said they, surely Satan hath tempted this bold neophyte to declare unholy and unheard of ways of finding truth contrary to all the teachings of the fathers. After many days more of grievous strife the dove of peace sat on the assembly, and they as one man, declaring the problem to be an everlasting mystery because of a grievous dearth of historical and theological evidence thereof, so ordered the same writ down.[1]

This story suggests a principle: *Turning to the Lord for help does not absolve us from turning to ourselves for that same help.* The Lord taught Oliver Cowdery this lesson in a different set of circumstances:

> Behold, the work which *you* [italics added] are called to do is to write for my servant Joseph. And, behold, it is because that you did not *continue* [italics added] as you commenced, when you began to translate, that I have taken away this privilege from you . . . . Behold, you have not understood; you have supposed that I would give it unto you [the

insights you need concerning your teaching], when you took no thought save it was to ask me. But, behold, I say unto you, that you must study it out in your mind [what is happening in your teaching]; *then* [italics added] you must ask me if it be right, and if it is right I will cause that your bosom shall burn within you; therefore, you shall feel that it is right. But if it be not right you shall have no such feelings, but you shall have a stupor of thought that shall cause you to forget the thing which is wrong. . . . Now, if you had known this you could have [received the insights into your teaching that were needed].[2]

Suppose, as outsiders, we come onto the scene of Allyson's teaching. What explanations can we offer? The first is obvious. She discounts the accumulation of her righteous intentions and personal goodness as she teaches week after week. Even though the class lacks open and personal participation, changes are occurring inside. Attitudes and values are being developed, as are testimonies, often unrealized by the girls themselves. Allyson has been set apart, is faithful to her calling, prepares carefully, and does the best she can. The Lord is magnifying her. Still, as we observe her classroom, we see that more good things could be happening.

We can turn to adolescent development for another explanation. These are normal 17 year-olds: dreamily romantic, anxious for peer approval, searching for personal identity, worried about school and life after graduation, trying to cope with their emerging womanhood, attracted to boys, and hopeful they will be asked to the prom. The Gospel is an important part of their lives, and they are developing testimonies.

The Church culture parallels their social culture. Beehives are gangling and goofy. Mia Maids are experiencing hormones and boys for the first time. Laurels are emerging young women who need to be cool, tolerant and polite around grownups—at least on the outside. Gushing over a lesson is beneath them; expressing sincere appreciation and sharing innermost feelings in a class are not yet comfortable experiences. Beyond all this, some may be unwilling, emotionally belligerent, antagonistic to the Gospel, and under duress. Some may be struggling with sin or with family estrangement.

Finally, other factors play into Allyson's "flat lessons." The approach to the lesson in the manual—having been created for a world-wide audience—may come across as wooden to these Laurels. The video which brings tears to an adult makes the girls roll their eyes. The "relevant" story is out of sync with their life in a modern American high school. They have heard and responded to the same questions a hundred times. The girls are probably not faulting the lessons or the doctrines within them; rather they simply feel no connection or involvement with them.

At this point Allyson's course is predictive: she spends more time and energy in preparing. With supplementary material stuffed into each lesson, she unwittingly becomes urgent, a sure way of closing down teenage girls.

Studying Your Teaching

Given a chance, the youthful friar would open the horse's mouth and count the teeth; Allyson, too, can turn a practical eye on her own teaching. We spontaneously study our teaching each time we replay a teaching episode in our minds, a process which may evoke a wide range of emotions: elation, quiet satisfaction, ho-humness, teary frustration, disappointment, emotional fatigue, or at times despondency. Our thoughts, as well, run the gamut: I tried to cover too much material, there was not enough variety, they loved my two stories, Brother Kohler is taking up too much class time, a few eyes lit up, I wonder if I over-prepared, I liked my drawings, too few people participated. Emotions and thoughts are triggered by classroom events and our perceptions of them. They spawn some self-correcting behaviors ("I'll not do that again!") and reinforce teaching patterns in others ("The way I'm preparing is working so well.").

To study your teaching is to ruminate about it, examine its nooks and crannies, employ a magnifying glass here and there, discover relationships among events, search outside information to better understand what is being discovered, and make decisions all along the way. Serious study beckons you across the entire terrain of your teaching, including but not limited to your inner self, your Gospel study, your purposes in teaching, your preparation, your relationships, and your methods. *The significance of self-study is that you, aided by the Spirit, are responsible for your own improvement.*

The thought of studying one's own teaching, turning inward, evokes at least two different reactions. First, teachers do not normally consider self-study to be part of their calling as teachers: "My time and energy are spent preparing and teaching. I don't have time to study my teaching." And from a different slant: "I've been called to teach, not to study myself doing it!" "If I try studying what I'm doing, I get pulled away from my real purpose, which is to teach." When set apart, a newly-called teacher is often counseled to "work to improve your teaching." This admonition is regularly interpreted by would-be teachers to mean reading Church materials and talks, as well as attending teacher in-service meetings—but not self-study.

Many teachers want to improve but see this approach as a bit too threatening:

> "It's hard enough trying to handle student comments about the lesson; asking them to help explore my teaching would be more than I could bear."

> "I'm already worried about my health, and I have to take my own blood pressure and blood sugar levels. What better way to add to my anxiety!"

> "I'm unsure of myself up there. Trying to study myself in that situation would be devastating."

A pedagogical nerve has been touched. The intensity of these reactions testifies of the potential of this approach. Unlike cosmetic changes, opening up one's teaching provides possibilities for deep-running improvement. Placing one's teaching under a personal microscope is frightening, yet it can be an awakening and invigorating experience. Some lament being in a "rut": unable to move forward, "doing the same old things week after week." Others have reached a plateau in their effectiveness and yearn for a new trajectory.

I have found teachers to be far more robust than they imagine. When invited and encouraged most are willing, many eager, to participate in self-study. Courage escalates quickly. Information about one's teaching can be gathered in many ways, one of which is videotaping. A teacher who is initially "unnerved" by teaching in front of a video camera often eagerly anticipates watching the rerun: "That's interesting. I'm more skillful in dealing with students than I thought." "Students are actually interested when we go to the scriptures. That surprises me." "I really do look comfortable in front of the class and I'm free from my notes." "I have to laugh at finishing students' sentences. My wife does it all the time, and I tell her it's a put down." "I hadn't realized how manipulative these kids are." "Good Grief! Look at the way I'm patronizing those kids. Come back in a couple of weeks and videotape me again. This has got to stop."

Expanding Awareness

Some years ago I conducted studies on teacher awareness, asking this fundamental question: What happens when we shine a "flashlight" into the corners of a person's teaching (video cameras, tape recorders, observations, interviews and other data-gathering devices)? The following results are relevant to our discussion:

1. As teachers became aware of events in their teaching—often involving dilemmas—the directing power of their past experience helped them to know what to do. Seldom did they seek help from others. On one occasion we videotaped two of a teacher's favorite students cheating on a midterm exam in the back of the room. On replay, the teacher blurted, "I can't believe this! I know exactly what I'm going to do." In this and other studies, teachers sat staring at the monitors witnessing themselves scolding students, calling on favored students more frequently, holding higher expectations for some students than others, acting self-conscious, being manipulated by students, telling too many jokes, displaying excellent handwriting skills, and exercising surprising competence. Many said, "I didn't realize I was doing that. I'm going to make some changes." Teachers who had had little formal teaching experience but had taught most of their lives in one arena or another had developed teaching instincts.

2. As awareness expanded, teachers were better able to identify possible consequences of their actions. This linking between what took place in the classroom and its *apparent* consequences on students was important to teachers. They were keenly interested in the consequences of what they did or said in the classroom: their activities, their questions, their handling of student comments, their methods. They were also concerned with how students affected each other. Allyson realized that the girls perceived her as aloof and, as a result, this was reciprocated by the girls' detachment; if she were to soften, so might they.

3. When teachers failed to make changes in their teaching, it was due more to lack of awareness than to lack of motivation. Teachers typically made changes in their teaching *once they were aware* that changes needed to be made. We could not expect Allyson to open up her humanness to the girls if she were unable to see a connection between their attitudes and her own.

Picture your awareness as a circle with you in the middle. You are aware of everything within the circle and little if anything outside it. As you gather information about your teaching the circle expands. The larger your circle of awareness, the greater your opportunities to reflect and make decisions: "Had I known about that I would have. . . ." "I never realized this was happening in my teaching." "I now see some new possibilities." Every person's teaching is a kaleidoscope of dynamic, inter–related, continually-changing events and circumstances.

Here is an example from my own teacher watching. Sitting near the back of the room in Priesthood meeting, I started observing both our instructor and the members of the class. Every time the teacher began preaching, scriptures came out, heads went down, and the brethren "escaped" from the lesson. (Why an instructor would preach to a group of 70 year-old saddle-broken saints is one of the mysteries of the Kingdom). As his preaching subsided and he embarked on a personal life experience, heads came back up and scriptures were set aside. This cycle occurred several times during our 40-minute class. The brethren were inadvertently signaling him to stop preaching. Were he aware of this connection, would his behavior have changed?

Suppose, as another example, a Mia Maid teacher enthusiastically presents a lesson on the importance of dieting to maintain good health. Would this well-meaning teacher have changed her approach had she known that Kelsey, sitting directly in front of her, was struggling with anorexia?

Returning to Allyson, we ask her to describe what is happening in her teaching from within her circle of awareness: "On any given Sunday, I can pull out maybe two or three comments from the girls; my stories create more interest than when we read the scriptures; when girls do comment, they don't volunteer much about their personal lives and struggles; they are interested in what each other is wearing; I think they think I'm too straight laced; they are not very comfortable with my style of teaching, and I often sense they tolerate being here because their parents want them in Church; conversations pick up once they leave class—they talk about the usual high school things; I truthfully don't know the state of their testimonies, I suppose most have them; we all seem to be going through the motions in class. They sit and I present lessons; I don't connect very well with them; they're quite different from each other; I guess Nichole is my best student; I get unnerved and sometimes angry when they sit during the whole time staring at me with emotionless expressions; when things are going poorly for me at home it shows in my teaching—I'm not very courteous and I sort of withdraw; girls can tell the days I don't want to be there; I'm often frustrated in preparing; overall I cannot really tell what kind of a job I'm doing, but I certainly don't see myself as very successful."

Allyson has described her awareness of her teaching terrain. Are there other inter–related events outside her awareness that might be important to her? She invites us to assist in this exploration. We observe, videotape, and interview students; information from our interviews is especially interesting. The five girls, interviewed as a group, report the following: About halfway through a lesson Allyson shifts to preaching, which causes the girls check out; her formal manner is interpreted as being guarded, aloof and unapproachable; but they also report that behind this "laced up" exterior she could be warm and giving; she probably cares for them but is unwilling or unable to express it; her lessons are not well tailored to their needs;

she is seen as a model of righteousness, obedience, and commitment to the Savior. If Allyson's circle of awareness were expanded to include these student perceptions, how would her inner self be reflected in her decisions?

At this point we perceive an important principle: *A teaching terrain is always open to further study. As new events enter a teacher's awareness, possibilities for change become apparent. The way in which we undertake change is influenced by the inner self.* Thus when Allyson becomes aware that her preaching closes students' ears, she is presented with a new possibility: stop preaching. Will her inner self allow it? When she becomes aware that students see her as guarded and aloof, a new possibility emerges: Relax, enter into their humanness with her own, and allow the girls into her life. Will her inner self allow it? Support it? From viewing the videotape she becomes aware of her preoccupation with presentation—would this explain why the girls are so quiet? What new possibility emerges? How will any changes she makes reflect her inner self?

A corollary follows: *New decisions offer additional opportunities for the Spirit to enter one's teaching.* Is Allyson willing to teach rather than preach, shed her protective formalism, allow her vulnerabilities to show, love more? These decisions—and a general change in her approach—cannot be undertaken without prayer.

Becoming Your Own Physician

The Church enlists one of the world's largest cadres of teachers. Consider the 25-35 required in every ward unit multiplied by the number of wards and branches throughout the Church. Add early morning and full-time Seminary teachers, volunteer and full-time Institute teachers, and CES missionary couples. Support and training personnel are stretched to the limit. In Utah Valley alone there are at least 82 volunteer stake Institute teachers, whose training is under the stewardship of three over worked administrators.

The Teaching The Gospel Course, occasional classroom visits, in-service mentors, manuals, and inspired talks by leaders all shore up and improve instruction in the home and Church. Yet each Sunday we enter and close the doors of our own classrooms. We are responsible for the quality of our teaching, answerable ultimately to our students and to the Spirit. Each of us becomes his or her own pedagogical physician.

Having considered the possibilities and power of studying your own teaching, two practical questions arise: How do I study my teaching? What aspects should I study—all of them?

[1] Quoted from C. E. Kenneth Mees, "Scientific Thought and Social Reconstruction," *General Electric Review*, 1934, p. 37, 113–119.
[2] Doctrine and Covenants 9: 4,5,6,10.

CHAPTER 4

METHODS FOR STUDYING YOUR TEACHING

Continuing the Story

Allyson, our seasoned but frustrated teacher, struggles with unresponsive 17 year-old girls. Suppose we are able to unobtrusively observe her teaching and note that she is following the principles of good teaching: uses pre–organizers; has good beginnings and endings in the lessons; gives applications and challenges; invites questions; makes good use of the chalkboard, videos, music and pictures. She follows the lessons in the manual, including stories, scriptures, and questions. The room temperature is regulated for comfort, chairs are arranged in circle, and a basket of Hersey's kisses sits alongside an attractive floral arrangement. After prayer and incidentals, Allyson moves briskly into the lesson with questions and scriptures inserted at the right spots. At the end comes an application: "How can a soft answer work with friends at school?" Then comes the challenge: "I want you to listen to your comments to others this week—to your friends and family members. See how often you can speak in a soft voice." Allyson bears testimony of soft answers in her own life. After the closing prayer the girls quietly file out. Frequently a girl will thank Allyson for the "good lesson" on her way out. Once in the hall, conversation springs to life—school, parties, dates, everything but the lesson.

Today is not unlike Sundays past. Alone, Allyson, pauses to take in the tastefully arranged table and the serene picture pinned to the cork strip. Only now does her body signal how drained it is from the last forty minutes. "I bop till I drop." She broods over the flatness of the lesson: "My preparations went so well this week. I got needed insights, and my lesson went as planned. But blah. Why am I batting my head against a wall? Sundays are an emotional wringer."

Leaving Allyson's classroom we infer at least one of her teaching beliefs: "If I prayerfully prepare and follow good techniques, the girls will absorb the lessons and grow in testimony." But a different reality confronts her, one understandably discouraging that sometimes leads to feelings of failure. The girls are unresponsive to her best efforts (as she sees it), but is she a failure or merely at the end of her vision? An important principle can be seen in Allyson's experience: *Much discouragement can be alleviated when teachers realize that "failure" is little more than not knowing what to do.* Although students have absolute veto power over their own learning and can blunt every attempt made in their behalf, teachers—Allyson included— can make changes which turn things around. The heartening message is that the majority of teachers need not live with "failure," a common nickname for lack of awareness. Too many teachers are quick to conclude: "That's just the way any students are" or, even more frightening, "That's just the way I am."

Happily, grit prevails. Having come from leathered pioneer stock, Allyson resolutely "straightens her shawl" while walking to her car. By mid afternoon life is back in focus, and these teenage fugitives are going to be reached. Allyson places a phone call not to Sister Thompson, the ward teacher improvement coordinator, but to Brian Vasquez, a high school teacher who lives in her ward. Sister Thompson has provided valuable library resources and support, but this time Allyson is in search of the workings of teenage girls.

Brian's days are filled with tumultuous teenage lives: urgent needs for peer acceptance, dislike of adult authority, caldrons of boiling hormones, emotional roller coasters, unbridled excitement, unrelieved boredom, and overfilled events and commitments. He listens intently to Allyson's problem, gradually smiling then giving in to hopelessly irreverant laughter. "I'm sorry. I don't mean any disrespect. But you have to understand I'm hearing your story from my world: I live with these kids every day. May I offer a suggestion. You're okay, and these girls are okay. Cut them some slack. Let them breathe in your classroom—and you breathe too. You're wound up tight like a spring. Without even sitting in your classroom, I'll wager you're an urgent teacher. Why not relax and enjoy these kids. I mean they're only teenagers trying to find out who they are. Warm up to them. You may be intimidating them. Beneath those fragile facades they're watching you like hawks. It won't be your lessons— it will be you. They need good models, and they need them now. Go ahead and be one—but be one they can relate to. These kids need real people more than they need carefully prepared lessons. They'll be okay. It's you I'm concerned about."

Allyson is reeling. She doesn't know whether to cry, laugh or get mad. All her agonizing, her hand wringing, and he cuts right through it.

"Every Sunday I come in stewing over these girls, and you tell me to relax and be human. That blows me away."

"Look, I'll bet I can go to every one of those girls and they'll tell me you're a good person, you teach good lessons, and you're committed to them. But they need *you*! Now don't misinterpret this, but maybe you need to spend a little less time on your knees and more time in their lives."

"Well, you *do* call it. I need time. I don't even know how to react to what you're saying. You're coming from a different world. I meet with these girls once a week. I wanted to know about teenage girls, and you've told me about me! You're basically saying I center too much on presenting lessons and not enough on relationships, that I'm not offering myself to them. Tell me, how would you react if someone said that to you?"

Allyson is confronted with an alternative view, one that surprises her. Metaphorically, Brian moved the ladder she was climbing to a different wall. In her climbing it had never occurred to her that the ladder might have been on the wrong wall. Her resolve was greater effort on the preparation wall; he moved the effort over to the relationship wall. *Allyson's awareness had been shifted: that is, expanded.* She is defensive, sobered, and enlightened, and, at the same time, she experiences a ripple of excitement.

Expanding Awareness Through Reflection

Brian leaves a somewhat bewildered Allyson. During their short visit he provoked her picture of her teaching, opened it up to potential realities she had previously not seen. Brian will not be available for follow-up consultation. She is left to her own thoughts about her teaching. But she is capable of carrying on without Brian (or others), of extending her own awareness by *reflection*. To "reflect" is to think carefully and exhaustively about something—for Allyson, her teaching. Reflection is self-study, becoming self-conscious of one's teaching in a particular setting. Like an out-of-body experience, we stand back and think about our inner selves, our preparation, our prayer, the Spirit at work, our delivery, the way we relate to students—the entire teaching terrain. *The goal of reflection is to expand our awareness, thereby opening up new and unthought—of possibilities for change.* It is the opening up of new possibilities that makes reflection so powerful. Reflection is a private activity which can be engaged in at any time either superficially or exhaustively. Invariably, good results occur.

Allyson reflects on Brian's observations: "Does he see me the way the girls see me?—maybe I do come across as anxious—urgent at times; but so what—the girls will understand my intentions—if I'm anxious, it's for *their* salvation—surely they can see that; suppose I were to try and relax more—would that bring them into the lesson? I may be overly concerned about the lesson itself—but does this mean I care less about them? no—but should I try to change in these areas?"

This sequence of reflection, with its questions, answers, conclusions, will eventually yield new insights, new awarenesses. Consider how we enlarge our understanding of the scriptures by pondering over them. We read 1st Nephi over and over and finally become aware that it is all about being with the Kingdom of God or being with the Kingdom of Satan. There is no middle ground: "Why didn't I see that? It was there all along! Only after pondering these chapters did I become aware of it." Allyson, too, will arrive at new awarnesses as she reflects on what Brian observed and on her own recollections of the past.

In the Church we are taught to reflect on the scriptures (feast), on our testimonies (testimony meetings), on our covenants (sacrament, temple), and on our family relationships (family home evening lessons). I was stunned when my three-year old granddaughter reported how she had learned to "search, ponder and pray" about the Book of Mormon in her Primary class!

Whatever form our reflection takes, the key is to engage in it. The process can be formalized to some extent with the following suggestions:

1. When an event has occurred, reflect back on it as soon as possible.
2. Continue to reflect on the event intermittently. This allows incubation to occur.

3. Use paper and pencil to enhance the process. Write about the experience.
4. Generate possible explanations: cause and effect relationships, consequences.
5. Make tentative decisions based on your reflections.
6. Pray for confirmation of those decisions.

Allyson's reflecting illustrates these six suggestions: (1) Brian's observations plagued her well into the night. (2) During the next few days the conversation kept returning to her mind. (3) She gave her thoughts tangible form by writing them: (4) Too much time on preparation, too little on relating to girls. What does that mean? I thought preparing *was* relating to them. Am I really too distant? If so why? Does it really have an effect upon the girls? Are the girls modeling my personality? Is that why they are aloof? Would girls really change if I changed? I kind of doubt it. "What they need is you." What did he mean? I am giving myself. How do teenage girls *need* a teacher? Why am I over-structured because I include everything in the manual? That doesn't make sense. I'm trying too hard. That doesn't make sense either. Sure I let others into my life, but not those I'm supposed to be teaching. Doctors don't do that when the treat patients. (5) I guess I'll try relaxing a little more, but this may throw me right into the fire. But I'm not going to slack off in my preparation—that would be a mistake. (6) Pray that relaxing is the best way to bless their lives.

Gathering Information To Reflect Upon

Unquestionably, Brian's conversation with Allyson increased her awareness of events that *might be* occurring in her teaching: for example, her tendency to be uptight was keeping the girls at bay. This is a good hunch. The scene to this point is similar to that encountered by our youthful friar: no one has looked in the mouth of the horse. Allyson must turn to the girls themselves for more direct evidence.

Hold on. Allyson was called to teach her students, *not* to solicit their help with her teaching. The nuance of credibility she has would surely evaporate. Think of their triumphant smiles: "We've got her now. She's getting desperate. She's coming to us. It's working." Allyson, like the rest of us, is pessimistic about the unknown.

The thought of intentionally collecting information about one's teaching generates resistance:

> "I was called to be a teacher to students for whom I have stewardship. My role is to prepare carefully and present good lessons; it is *not* to go out and gather information about my teaching, an activity that would eat up my precious time and energy."

> "We all know we can improve as teachers, so why bring out a microscope."

> "What is to be gained by scratching around in my teaching? I'm being led astray from my fundamental charge."

> "The thought of studying my teaching frightens me. I am not secure enough to do it."

These are fair criticisms from competent teachers. The serviceable philosophy is if it works, don't fix it. When a teacher reaches a plateau of effectiveness, there is no pressing reason for change. Yet there is still the lurking question: How much better could good teachers be if they studied their teaching?

Curiosity is pulling Allyson out of her comfort zone. "What if Brian is right? Do I have the courage to find out?" One Sunday she finishes her lesson ten minutes early, then asks the girls if they would help her on a project. She passes out paper and pencils and writes two questions on the chalkboard: "What happens in the class to open up your learning?" "What happens to close it down?" To her surprise, all the girls immediately begin writing—like an assignment at school! She collects the papers and tucks them away in her folder. Later, with her study door closed, she pulls out the papers. Allyson can't help but chuckle at her pounding heart. Why is this so threatening? She begins to read. Some responses are complete, others superficial. But the girls have actually volunteered their reactions! To the first question she reads, "When you laugh (which isn't often)," "When you let your hair down," "When you become human too," "When you tell personal stories," "When a scripture or story has personal meaning for you," "When the lesson is interesting," "When you *slow down*!" To the second question, the girls had answered, "When the lesson doesn't relate to me," "When I feel you're preaching at me," "When you ask questions I've heard for the last 100 years," "When you act as if we all feel the way you do," "When the lesson is boring." Allyson broodingly folds the papers neatly in a stack. "Well, I asked them and they told me; my connecting with them is *really* important; well they're honest and respect me enough to reveal their feelings—that's good; I need to let them into my life-sounds like they would respond better to the lessons if I did; how interesting—who I am affects my teaching."

Several weeks later Allyson comes early to class and sets up a tape recorder to record her lesson and the girls' participation. "What's the tape recorder for?" "I'm studying my teaching and want to hear myself." At first there is self-consciousness as the girls know the tape recorder is running; but hesitation soon melts away as the lesson proceeds. No one cares by the lesson's end. Home in her study, pencil in hand, Allyson replays the tape, jotting down a note here and there:

> You're finishing their sentences for them!
> Wonderful! I vary my activities. I like that.
> Hmm—now, half way through, I start preaching. They told me it turns them off. Why do I do that?
> Megan must have gotten focused enough to ask the question—I seem to be almost scolding in my reply to her—that's surprising.
> Laura was trying to tell me something—stop assuming all of us have testimonies like yours.
> I keep pressing Nichole to say something. Why do I find it important to get her to talk?
> I'm asking all the questions—then I answer them!
> I'm urgent—trying to engineer their thinking and feelings—but in a good sort of way.
> Brian is uncanny. How did he see all this?
> Well prepared—my presentation went smoothly—I like that.

Allyson turns off the recorder and moves to the window. Fresh new buds are appearing on the apple tree. She gazes at them for a long time. "Teaching is so complex—I'm beginning to think preparation is only a small part; how naive—I'm beginning to understand their guardedness—I've been secretly blaming them for not responding; I'm sending all kinds of messages. Who I love and don't like—maybe I should have remained in my blissful state."

A month later Allyson has a video camera set up as the girls walk in. Again there is some wariness as the girls sense a film being produced. Allyson leaves the camera pointed on herself, which is a relief for the girls. As with the audiotape recorder, the fact that the camera is running soon becomes insignificant. Later in the day Allyson plays the tape in her VHS. Again her heart is pounding. How frightening to actually see yourself teaching! But her eyes become riveted to the monitor as she picks up every movement, every expression, every statement. Listening to the whir of rewinding, a slow smile begins to form: "I can't believe I'm doing this—actually watching myself teach; so this is how others see me when I teach—I'm seeing more on a forty-minute videotape than I could have ever imagined; now, replay it—put it on pause—take notes—what is happening?"

Allyson ponders the notes she took during a second run through: "I'm putting up a protective shield when I walk in there—I'm really a warmer person than I see here; I like the way I dress, and I like my presentation—it's impressive—even to me; but I wonder—could my super lessons be a way of holding students at bay? Brian's right—I'm quite uptight—kind of stiff—looks like I'm afraid the girls will question what I have to teach; why am I afraid of that—I don't want to look dumb—not knowing the answers; I seem to enjoy what I'm doing—wonder if the girls can see that; its clear I walk on eggs with Laura—am I afraid she'll leave? It's obvious—Tamara's my favorite—the girls can see that—wonder why; yes, I pressure Nichole—I've got to stop that—its okay if she doesn't participate; why can't I connect with Tosha? How does she see me? This tape is nerve racking—painful may be a better word; but I must admit, there are some new things here—the direction is clear—it's kind of exciting—but I may not be able to change—I'd have to do something new—awfully insecure; what if I really could relax and enjoy the girls? What would happen if I opened up? Wow—maybe they'd think I want to be one of them—then I'd be in trouble; this could be fun—is that what my calling's supposed to be?—fun—well, at any rate—

it's clear I judge my success on how well the lesson presentation went—pulling girls into a discussion is also important to me—I can see also that I feel a need to cover everything in the lesson—Hmm."

These three information-gathering procedures, simple as they are, allow Allyson to actively explore her teaching terrain. Her expanded awareness of herself, her teaching and her relationships offers new possibilities for reflection, choices and decisions, and involvement of the Spirit. For example, her agenda—well-oiled presentations which cover the material in the lesson in a timely manner- has never considered agendas the girls might have. Worrying about whether you will be invited on the hay ride with the popular kids, though trivial from an eternal perspective, may seem more desperate than "Learning to Speak Soft Words." Further, let's presume Allyson decides to experiment by vacating her comfort zone and yielding to her whisperings to relax, open up, and share her humanness. She yearns to be able to connect with these girls by allowing them inside her life. Picture their reaction as she does so. They receive permission—an invitation—to likewise be open and vulnerable. Now *real* teaching can begin: transformation of both teacher and student. Those lessons, so rigidly prepared and presented, are recast to feed and inspire the girls, who are now more susceptible to them. Allyson, responding to new information and promptings, changes herself and thereby her teaching with positive results. She has burst out of a monotonous plateau to a new level of effectiveness.

I currently teach in the Stake Institute Program; my students are an ebullient group between the ages of 18 and 30. Following is an example of reflection in my own teaching:

One Wednesday night we were reading 1st Nephi 1: 9-10. Father Lehi was invoking metaphors to urge his sons Laman and Lemuel to soften their hearts and follow the counsels of the Lord. To Laman he said, "O that thou mightest be like unto this river, continually running into the fountain of all righteousness," and to Lemuel, a verse later, "O that thou mightest be like unto this valley, firm and steadfast, and immovable in keeping the commandments of the Lord."

I invited the class to take two or three minutes and think of a metaphor their fathers might use in wishing for them: "I wish you were like a . . . . " Silence. After the time period, still silence. None could create a personal metaphor. I gave them an assignment for the coming week: "Keep thinking about a metaphor Mom or Dad would select. Talk with them if you like."

Then we moved to verse 11, where I pointed out the relationship between stiffneckedness and murmuring. I had decided beforehand to ask for adjectives describing "stiffneckedness," then to tell a story nailing down the concept. Class members came up with descriptors such as *cocky, prideful, hardened heart, inflexible, cannot hear.* With these words before us, I told the story to provide an image. Many years ago in Australia, my companion and I roomed in a home with an outside privy situated some twenty yards from the home. Each time we made our way to the little house, we were accosted by a "stiffnecked" rooster who claimed squatters' rights to the path. He would wait until we were walking away from him to mount his leg-pecking attack at full speed. After a week of flesh wounds on our calves, we decided to "humble" him. I positioned myself behind the privy with a bucket of cold water while my companion served as bait. As the scene unfolded with the rooster charging in hot pursuit, my companion stepped deftly to the side allowing the rooster to absorb the full barrage of gushing water. The Magnum force blasted him off the path. Regaining his feet, totally drenched, he strutted stiffneckedly back to his house.

Following our class and throughout the late evening I felt restive. In spite of comments from students that our time had been well spent, I was troubled. Rehearsing our hour together several times, I came to two conclusions. First, I realized that an assignment to simply ask parents for descriptive metaphors served no useful purpose. Unless presented in a useful way, it would be of no uplifting value to the student. Second, the Australian rooster story, though a comic relief, carried no redeeming value. I had described a rooster's behavior, but this had contributed nothing to our understanding of stiffneckedness as a form of pride, nor had it suggested why Lehi would have used the word. Further reflecting made me aware that these aspects of the lesson did not contribute to our understanding or feelings about Lehi's relationship to his sons. In continued reflection, I realized I had tried too hard to make the chapter meaningful; I had only made it less meaningful. In the midst of personal reflection, the Spirit had whispered to me.

Let us summarize, then, what it means to study your teaching: *(1) gathering information, (2) reflecting, (3) making changes—*

repeating the cycle. This cycle, engaged in regularly, constitutes the study of your teaching.

Using Varied Information Sources

The opportunities to gather information about your teaching are limited only by your imagination. Weigh the following possibilities: simple questionnaires and response sheets (see Appendix A), tape recordings, videotapings, individual student and group interviews, benevolent observers, and a teaching journal. One ingenious Seminary teacher passed out a student response sheet with two columns headed "Tuned in?" "Tuned out?" Down the left side were numbered rows 1 through 30. Every few minutes, after discussing a concept or after reading a passage, he paused and clicked a "cricket," and voiced a number (e.g. "13"), signaling each student to check either "Tuned in" or "Tuned out" at that number. About 18-25 clicks occurred at strategic points throughout the lesson. With a tape recorder playing near his voice, the instructor was able to synchronize how students were responding internally to what he was teaching, when what he said or did caused them to "tune in" or "tune out." His results showed that attention picked up during personal stories and declined upon returning to the scriptures.

Experimentation will help you develop skill in exploring your terrain. Your interest, your courage, and your willingness are the greatest challenges to be faced. My work with teachers repeatedly shows that when the desire is present, many different ways are created to gather information. Like Allyson, teachers are invariably surprised at the willingness of their students to participate in an improvement program. When their help is solicited, they can be honest, introspective and insightful. They respect a teacher's desire to understand what happens inside students and are relieved in not having to judge the teacher's effectiveness.

Further explanation is in order on this last point. Recall that Allyson passed out sheets of paper and asked the girls to respond to two questions: "What happens in the class to open up your learning?" "What happens to close it down?" These questions are very different from "Am I a good teacher?" "How effective am I in helping you grow?" and "What am I doing well and what do I need to improve?" If she had asked these latter three questions, Allyson would be asking students *to make judgements of her*. In the two she did hand out, she asked students *to make judgements of themselves*. The difference is significant. On the basis of what students report about themselves (e.g. "I open up my learning when you let your hair down.") *she*—the teacher—assesses her effectiveness. Thus in the two questions she asked, Allyson gathered information that informed her, rather than having the students evaluate her teaching. What teachers need to learn from students is what opens and closes their learning; the teachers themselves make decisions about what to change. Using students as a source of information rather than as evaluators calms teachers' reluctance to approach students for help.

Simple questionnaires, tape recordings and videotapes have been illustrated in Allyson's study of her teaching. Several other methods will be briefly described.

<u>Student Interviews</u>

Experienced elementary, middle and high school teachers are a marvel to observe. One day I was sitting in on a fourth-grade class in which basic math concepts were being taught. Students were lethargic and off task. The teacher stopped and said, "We are having trouble today. Let's talk about why our minds are not working properly." Immediately hands went up. "It's the long weekend," "This is too hard," "I can't help it," "I just want to get up and run," "It's raining outside." I observed a similar strategy by an English teacher in an advanced placement class: "homecoming," "spring break," "the pep rally," and "the big dance" were students' responses.

With care, Church teachers can conduct productive whole-class interviews, especially teachers who are responsible for youth, teenagers and young adults. These interviews must not degenerate into gripe sessions; they should be opportunities to find out what is happening inside students when we "do class." The atmosphere needs to be safe and open, and students must stay focused on themselves. It is a diagnostic rather than a remedial session: "I get excited when . . . ." "When one or two people monopolize the talk I check out. . . ." "I relate more to scriptures than to interesting archeological findings."

Less risky are small group or individual student interviews: again, most helpful with intermediate age groups. Trust and openness must be first developed. Allyson's interviews might seem destined to painfully awkward silences. But one never knows. Individual interviews may be the very vehicle for the development of openness. As Allyson visits in her home, Laura cannot help but see a commitment in her teacher, an earnest attempt to connect with her life. At first their conversation about school, work, and other challenges is terse and stilted. But Laura may decide she can trust Allyson and open up to her. Whatever the result, Allyson leaves with impressions about how to approach Laura through her teaching.

A Benevolent Observer

An underused but fruitful ally is an observer. Teachers mistakenly assume that (1) outside observers will "evaluate" their teaching and (2) observers must be trained to be helpful. Allyson calls up a friend:

> "Would you mind coming into my class next Sunday and sitting in the back. I will hand you a paper and pencil. All you have to do is write down everything you see happening in my class during the 40-minute period."
>
> "Why me? I don't know anything about teaching. How can I come in and evaluate you?"
>
> "I don't want you to evaluate me—I'll do that. You are simply my observer, my video camera recording the event."
>
> "Why don't you just bring in a videotape camera?"
>
> "Because I want the events recorded through human eyes. You will notice things you think are worth describing, and you will make inferences about cause and effects. For example, suppose you notice that students seem to be off task during some parts of the lesson and you think to yourself, 'These girls get bored when she goes through so many scriptures on the same point.' Sometimes you will write down just what you see: for example, 'Megan keeps passing notes to Tamara.' At other times you will write down an inference: for example, 'I think the pace is too fast; trying to cover too much territory.' Everything you write is fine. Go ahead,

write whatever comes to mind. Then at the end of class hand me the paper as you walk out. I'll take it home and reflect on what you have written. The main suggestion is to write as much as you can during the class."

"Well, if that's all you want I can do it—but remember I'm not a trained teacher."

Obviously, an observer coming into a class of five teenage girls is going to upset the dynamics more than going into a class of ten or into a large adult class. But no matter. Allyson will have plenty to reflect on. She is using a friend to gather information about her teaching.

Several years ago when I started using observers in my research, I trained them carefully to observe detailed and intricate aspects of a person's teaching. Observations were clearly separated from inferences. While data gathered by a trained observer is more complex, detailed and definitive than those from an untrained person, even one with little experience provides enough to make the activity worthwhile. I have discovered that "naive" observers can provide a remarkable amount of information while sitting through a class with the simple instruction to keep writing. Teachers who become skillful at reflecting can productively use even the most elementary observations. In my research, I found the challenge is not lack of training on the observer's part but lack of willingness on the teacher's part.

A Teaching Journal

I have asked people why they keep personal journals: "So I can go back and see how much growth I've made," "It's my therapist," "We've been commanded to," "I want a record of my experiences in life," "It helps me find out who I really am," "It helps me know what changes I need to make in my life."

A teaching journal provides similar results. Descriptions of teaching episodes—with their accompanying feelings of success and failure, false starts and great endings, and student reactions, as well as the teacher's desires and commitments to change—represent good sources of information. *To write in a journal about one's teaching is to reflect on one's teaching.* One of the assignments given to student teachers during the time they practice in the schools is to keep a teaching journal. When interviewed at the end of this experience, they report that referring to a journal allows them "to see the mistakes [they've] made" and "to write down the changes [they] want to make."

This journal need not be time consuming, nor must it be written in elegant detail. A simple notebook where ideas, impressions, and suspected cause and effect relationships can be jotted down is sufficient. Teachers find it useful to have the journal in front of them as they prepare subsequent lessons.

These methods, along with any number of others, help you generate information about your own teaching as it occurs in your classroom. Studying the teaching of others—as well as the suggestions of others—almost always triggers reflection on your own teaching. To that we now turn.

CHAPTER 5

STUDYING OTHER TEACHERS

Expanding The Picture

This book began with a basic premise: *Who one is and how one teaches are dynamically related.* Method is the instrument through which the inner self is expressed. Maximal Improvement comes by increasing goodness and by the study of your teaching. Chapter 2 was devoted to the inner self: its spiritual characteristics, its natural-man tendencies, and the changes which can occur through repentance. Scriptures and Gospel knowledge have contributed to our understanding of the inner self. In Chapter 3 we turned attention to the second part of the premise: the study of your teaching. To that aspect I have tried to bring a sensitive rendering of secular knowledge, primarily empirical data gathered from research and from theoretical orientations in the field. We learned how study of one's own teaching increases awareness and opens up new possibilities for change. In Chapter 4 we studied methods for studying your teaching. The purpose of this chapter is to expand your awareness through the study of *others'* teaching.

Suppose we come upon Sister Sanchez, a Sunday School teacher. Her inner self literally radiates through her lessons—authenticity, meekness, selflessness, and love. Yet her 13 year-olds are "coming off the walls, passing notes, switching seats, making wise cracks, darting in and out for bathroom visits, and bursting into laughter at whispered comments." Though the classroom ambiance is loving, it's chaotic. Her friends offer their reactions:

> "Well, this kind of a saint gets eaten alive. She should never have been sentenced to work with teenagers—too nice; kids will trample all over her."

> "You don't try to change wonderful women like this; she ought to be serving as Compassionate Service Leader in Relief Society."

"Her level of spirituality is too high for these kids to appreciate; she needs rescuing."

"She could never develop the 'look of death'."

We all know of such saints who are challenged to the limit in reaching teenagers. At first glance, their gifts seem to lie elsewhere, not with teaching teenagers. Repenting, shedding the natural man, and purifying one's inner self does not, by itself, insure good teaching. What more can Sister Sanchez do? Surely she does not need to develop a more Christlike inner self.

It is *because* of her willing inner self that Sister Sanchez, once she becomes aware of classroom events and their consequences, can (will) effect changes in her teaching. Indeed, my research suggests that most teachers, saints or otherwise, welcome the opportunity to make changes—from small corrections to abrupt turnarounds-when they can see the possibility of new results.

Life in classrooms is a complex set of interrelationships. In crossing this panorama, we will stop here and there in this chapter to observe and reflect upon these relationships, hopefully increasing your awareness of relationships in your own teaching.

Examining Styles of Teaching

Across a random sample of church classrooms, one observes relatively limited variety in teaching styles—presumably because most teachers grow up in the same Church teaching culture. Following are styles we commonly see.

Review Teaching

This style is deeply embedded in our culture, and few teachers think consciously of its characteristics and results. Typically, the teacher moves through the lesson by asking the class a series of questions which call for factual information learned at an earlier time. The questions often chronicle a story as it appears in the scriptures:

"Why did Lehi and his family leave Jerusalem?"
"After they left, what were the sons instructed to return and do?"

"How long did the family wander in the wilderness near the borders of the Red Sea?"
"Who can relate the broken bow incident?"
"How did Nephi build the ship?"
"Once out to sea, what happened aboard ship?"

Review teaching can be adopted to a variety of topics:

"Who is in charge of missionary work in the ward?"
"What can we do to find people to teach?"
"What do we know about Luke?"
"Would someone tell us the story of Jonah?"
"What commandments were Adam and Eve given in the Garden?"
"Who can describe how the Liahona worked?"
"Let me read Luke 6:13: 'And when it was day he called unto him his disciples: and of them he chose twelve, whom also he named as apostles.' Let's list them on the board."

Procedurally, the teacher asks the question (or makes a fill-in-the blank statement), then students volunteer answers. Students often confirm, add to, amplify, or correct responses given by other students or the teacher. Almost never is the entire class baffled by a question; someone always knows the answer. When differences of opinion arise, students rely on various sources of authority to authenticate their responses:

"I've always been taught..."
"Elder McConkie says in *Mormon Doctrine*..."
"All the evidence leads to this conclusion."
"I have a note in my scriptures that says..."

Interspersed among questions, the teacher presents scriptures, a story, a personal experience. These on-route "pauses" often evoke related stories and experiences from class members. At the end of the lesson the teacher usually summarizes what is written in the manual and bears testimony about the lesson.

Results of review teaching. Teachers report they like this kind of teaching: "It gets the class involved" and "I don't have to do all the talking." They further report that students will feel motivated to read the lesson before coming to class in order to participate in the discussion. Review teaching requires relatively little preparation time since the questions (and sometimes desired student responses) are listed in the manual, as are the scriptures and stories. Finally, teachers feel success when "the class becomes involved." Students sitting through this style of teaching offer a variety of reactions:

> "It's good to keep reviewing what we've already learned—people learn by repetition."

> "I'm generally familiar with what we talk about but often come away with one or two new insights."

> "I like to be able to give answers."

> "You feel like you can jump in with your two-cents worth."

> "I don't learn anything new—I'm not sure why I go."

Youth reactions are typically less positive:

> "It's okay, I guess."

> "Pretty boring."

> "Wish she'd teach us something new."

Commentary on review teaching. The scriptures offer ample proof of the importance of recalling and remembering:

> I would that ye should do as I have done, in remembering the captivity of our fathers.[1]

> I have always retained in remembrance [our fathers] captivity; yea, and ye also ought to retain in remembrance, as I have done, their captivity.[2]

Rememberest thou the covenants of the Father unto the house of Israel?[3]

Our modern leaders, as well, talk of repetition. For example, Elder Maxwell has commented, "Some of life's hardest lessons require repetition."[4]

At least one reason this style of teaching is so prevalent, then, is that "remembering" (repetition) is an admonition woven not only through the words of the scriptures and our modern leaders, but throughout our Church curricula as well.

But there is a second, less justified reason for the prevalence of review teaching among teachers: inadequate Gospel study and lesson preparation on the part of the teacher. Gospel review is always helpful, but if *no new insights or deeper understandings result,* then growth proceeds slowly and sporadically.

The advantages of review teaching are meager. Students spend most of their time reviewing what they already know—and few we have interviewed expect much more than this from their attendance. In class after class, the same few people do most of the talking at all age levels. We have occasionally observed that less thoughtful members do most of the volunteering, while more thoughtful members close down and withdraw into silence. But the most serious drawback is that review teaching falls short in elevating Gospel understanding to the level urged by our leaders. Insights and understanding students acquire—or are motivated to acquire—are not comparable to the seat time invested. Gospel instruction must increase understanding rather than merely stamp in factual information long since learned. It is enlarged understanding more than a storehouse of facts that motivates behavior change.

As the inner self awakens through thoughtful repentance, at least two favorable things happen: (1) focus on casual presentation gives way to a "sincere anxiety" about constant student growth, and (2) deeper preparation ensues. Both of these changes pull the teacher out of review teaching and into a unique style which leads students from a maintenance level to a growth level.

Re–conversion teaching

Parallel to review teaching, re–conversion teaching attempts to re–convert students to that which they already believe. Well meaning, the teacher fails to consider the nature of the students for whom the lesson is intended. Following are several examples:

A group of scout leaders who have dedicated their time, resources and energies to the building of young men are attending a district roundtable where the teacher passionately challenges, "Do you know the worth of a boy?"

Dedicated volunteer Seminary teachers who are attending a Church Education System conference hear the teacher implore, "Can we impress upon you how important your role is in directing the youth of this Church."

A class of covenant-keeping, Sabbath-respecting members are presented with a lesson titled "Observing the Sabbath" in which they are urged to keep the Sabbath.

A group of returned missionaries are presented with a lesson on the Apostasy during which the teacher fills the lesson with scriptures showing there was indeed an apostasy.

When interviewed, teachers explained their re–conversion teaching as follows:

"I've been so busy preparing my lesson it never occurred to me to think about what my students already believe about it."

"I teach the lesson as outlined in the manual; I don't worry about anything else."

"I don't worry about it because whether they believe it or not its good to keep reviewing things over and over."

Results of re–conversion teaching. Students vary in their reactions. Some like to be reminded about what they believe; but greater numbers of them open their scriptures, start whispering, ask unrelated questions, attempt detours, or simply tune out and think about other things, returning now and then to the lesson presentation. Interest and attention tend to fade whenever student's reaction is, "I already believe that."

Commentary on re–conversion teaching. The scriptures admonish intense conversion: "But that I might more fully persuade them to believe in the Lord their redeemer."[5] But deeper conversion and re–conversion are different concepts. Re–conversion means to start over, to go through the same process again; deeper conversion means to go beyond what has already taken place. Notice the difference in these two student comments: "I am already converted to that principle and, as a result, I'm going to think about something else," as compared to "I am becoming more deeply converted to that principle; I will continue my thinking." Re–conversion teaching evokes the first response; going beyond evokes the second.

Advancing beyond review teaching tends to solve as well the tendency to engage in re–conversion teaching. Both of these styles of teaching result from sleepiness of the inner self and lack of awareness of classroom events; the result of either is a lack of seriousness in teacher focus and preparation. If teachers are to take students to new levels of understanding that invite stronger conversion, they themselves must lead the way.

Urgent Teaching

Sometimes a teacher who is eager to keep youth on the straight path to or move others briskly toward salvation, becomes too brisk- urgent, insistent, pressing. Such teaching intentionally imposes upon the student's agency. *Anxiously* engaged in a good cause, the teacher becomes too anxious:

"I *really* want you to feel how important this is."

"I just feel so strongly about the importance of this!"

"This affects your eternal welfare!"

"Maybe if I try hard enough they'll see its importance."

"I'm in the save-them-at-all-costs club and I can't help myself."

In our interviews with students (especially youth) the following types of comments occur:

"We'll give her an A for effort!"

"She surely believes it—I applaud her for that."

"When he comes on too strong I bail out."

"I wish she'd realize our testimonies are not as strong as hers."

Results of urgent teaching. Our interviews suggest that youth and adults tend to tune out when teachers become urgent and anxious to the extent that their teaching lacks serenity. When students feel their agency intruded upon, they resist the teacher's intentions, worthy though they might be. When teachers sense they are "losing the class," urgency escalates, more students escape, and the cycle tightens.

Commentary on urgent teaching. Urgent teaching takes its toll on the teacher; she is literally exhausted at the end of a class period. Many if not most teachers are urgent as they experience the responsibility of their calling and are thus unable to completely relax with students. But some become intensely urgent because they feel guilty over their lack of preparation and attempt to compensate- wanting to promote in students the same motivation they might have generated had they been well prepared.

Repentance emancipates teachers, frees them to relax; so also does thorough preparation. Relaxed teachers give a more credible message because they are more credible themselves.

Preaching

Urgency soon blossoms into preaching. Voice intensifies, pitch goes up, sometimes scolding occurs, and challenges are liberally meted out. In my interviews with teachers, few have been satisfied with the effects of their preaching: "I overdid it." "Maybe I shouldn't have finished like that, but I have such strong feelings about this." "I get the feeling students don't like to be preached to, so why do I keep doing it?" Following are examples from the hallways of our classrooms:

> "Are we without sin in this valley?"

> "Do you allow improper videos into your homes?"

> "Are you prepared to stand before the judgement bar this very day?"

> "Can we justify shopping on the Sabbath?"

Results of preaching. Some students report feeling "cleansed," happy to have been "called to repentance." For most, however, a little preaching goes a long way, and students rapidly "check out" on the teacher. On videotapes we have observed intentional sleeping, reading scriptures in adult classes, and withdrawal posture in teenage classes. Teenagers talking, passing notes, and laughing are resistance messages sent to the teacher. Comments like the following can be picked up:

> "When a teacher starts preaching at me, I'm out of here!" (Youth)

> "I don't mind being talked at once in a while, but *every* Sunday?"

> "I need to be called to repentance once in a while—and I appreciate him doing so."

> "Why does she have to keep preaching to us?"

Commentary on preaching. "Exhortation" is a legitimate activity for teachers. The distinction between exhortation and preaching may be in motive: the former carried out in tenderness and love, and the latter, in scolding. A more fruitful distinction, however, is between "teaching" and "preaching." In General Conference, the

Brethren and Sisters teach us rather than preach to us—good models to follow.

In classrooms, a pattern can be observed: Insufficient preparation very often leads to preaching, as it does to urgent teaching. Well-prepared teachers seldom engage in preaching because their message, carefully developed, renders its own power. Ill-prepared teachers feel a pressure to motivate; well prepared teachers motivate naturally.

Again a repenting inner self finds expression. Greater authenticity, respectfulness, and compassion disallow preaching. Gentle suggestions rather than unrelenting and strident challenges come from a resolved inner self.

Direct Teaching

With this style the teacher does most of the talking: presenting, explaining, demonstrating. Students occasionally break in with questions and comments, often a short interchange ensues, and the teacher resumes. Direct teaching occurs more in Relief Society and Young Women than in the Melchizedek Priesthood classes. Our data show that women consistently prepare more extensively than men, thus generating more material for their teaching. In preparation for teaching youth, Primary teachers log more hours than Aaronic Priesthood advisors, and surveys of youth Sunday School teachers show differences between male and female teachers. Teachers who engage in greater preparation do more of the talking, which explains why more direct teaching occurs among the sisters.

Following are comments from teachers using this style:

"I spend a lot of time preparing."

"New insights come slowly, and I have to work for them."

"I've prepared some important things to say, and I want to say them."

"I really love to teach this class."

"I sort of wish I weren't doing all the talking—but I don't think I want to change."

"I don't think class members mind listening if I have something worthwhile to say."

Here is a sample of the types of student responses:

"I don't feel I want to jump in as much; she has worked so hard to prepare."

"Sometimes I want to make a comment, but I feel I'd pull him off track."

"I like it because we're not hearing a lot of irrelevant comments from class members."

"She gives you lots to think about. " (youth)

"I usually come away feeling my time has been well spent."

"I appreciate how carefully he prepares."

"I got bored because she was just standing up there talking at me."

Results of direct teaching. Considerably more information can be dispensed during 40 minutes in a direct teaching classroom. The well-prepared teachers we interviewed felt quite comfortable using this approach, while the less prepared feared running out of material before the end of class. Student reactions vary, some feeling they are not given an opportunity to express thoughts and feelings, and others breathing a sigh of relief. In general, students feel their time is well spent when they are directly instructed by a knowledgeable teacher. They feel less of a need to contribute or participate verbally when the teacher has something worthwhile to say, especially when new insights and interpretations are achieved. Direct instruction by poorly prepared teachers inevitably leads to student boredom.

Commentary on direct teaching. A prevailing and even gnawing fear with direct teaching is that "students won't feel part of the lesson." Discouraging participation is an accusation to which teachers do not want to feel guilty. But this worry is misplaced. With strong preparation and sensitive teaching, student "participation" takes care of itself. Rather than jumping in, students will ask and think with deliberation. Silence does not indicate lack of involvement; indeed, the opposite is often the case. The air need not always be full of talk. Thorough preparation, regardless of teaching style, evokes thought—let thought be participation.

Once again, teaching is a public expression of the inner self. Repentance awakens greater feelings of responsibility which, in turn, draw the teacher toward intensity of preparation—which may or may not lead to a direct style of teaching.

Conversation Teaching

Some teachers have a conversational style to their teaching. The teacher makes several comments then turns to the group and says in effect, "Shall we talk about this?" or "What is your thinking on this?" or "Let's talk back and forth about this scripture." There is an exchange of ideas, thinking, testimonies, stories. Conversation teaching differs from review teaching in that rather than reviewing what students know through a series of questions, the teacher says, "Here is my best thinking about King Benjamin as a model for fathers—what is yours?" Then, after some exchange, the teacher says, "Are we ready to move now to the effect of his talk?" Meandering is more common here than with review teaching.

Results of conversation teaching. Teachers using this style like the more relaxed and unstructured way of relating the subject to the students. More structured teachers shun this approach, preferring a faster pace and greater control over the lesson. Conversational teachers do not appear to prepare as intensely for the lesson itself but are often well enough versed in the Gospel to call upon their background in responding to students and leading the discussion.

Students differ in their reactions. Some thrive on "think time" during the lesson, moving from one idea to the next in a leisurely fashion. Others become frustrated with the lack of structure and feel time is being wasted.

<u>Commentary on conversation teaching</u>. This approach is not common in the Church teaching culture and, for that reason, perhaps is less popular with students. It takes greater account of student interests and needs, but runs a greater risk of getting out of sync, not so much with lesson content as with pacing over the year. Conversational teachers are more likely to discuss peripheral topics relating to the lesson.

This style reveals a relaxed inner self, one respectful of personal agency although less urgent in moving students toward salvation.

Hurry-up Teaching

A disadvantage of individual lessons covering so much material is that teachers feel pressure to blaze through a lot of lesson content. This acceleration can occur over the entire lesson or can be reserved for a burst of speed as the hour draws to an end with miles yet to travel. Following are examples of teacher comments which result from the pressure to move through too much material:

"An interesting comment but we need to get back on the lesson."

"We don't really have enough time to cover everything I want to cover."

"I will just touch upon the differences between Martha and Mary then we have to move on."

The teacher's responses to students and even to lesson content are affected as well:

A class discussion arises about temple-going saints who leave much to be desired in their business dealings. The discussion becomes more intense. The teacher jumps in and calls a halt: "Now this whole class cannot be devoted to this subject—we have four more to cover!"

A student offers a comment while the teacher rummages through his notes, responds with "Thank you for that comment," then races forward.

The story of the Good Samaritan is being discussed, and the teacher soon interrupts with "Oh, you know the story—we don't need to talk about it in detail."

The teacher offers a thought-provoking question then moves on without allowing students to either think about it or respond.

Results of hurry-up teaching. Almost always students feel put off by a teacher racing through the lesson material, more intent on "covering everything" than on actually teaching. Here are typical student reactions to this type of teaching:

"I like moving this quickly—we cover a lot of ground."

"We hardly have time to think or digest before the teacher has moved on to something else."

"I wish we'd go at a more leisurely pace. I don't feel I learn that much."

"The teacher has so much to cover we skip superficially across the top, never getting down to some new ideas."

Commentary on hurry-up teaching. This hurried type of teaching results from unrealistic expectations about how much teaching can occur in 35-40 minutes. Attempting seven chapters in Second Nephi, though recommended in the manual, is unrealistic. The pressure felt by teachers to cover all seven chapters forces them into superficial coverage. Further, our data show that students check out when teachers accelerate their teaching. Teachers have difficulty selecting two or three concepts or principles and lovingly setting the rest aside.

Again, the inner self generates the outer response: As teachers shift focus from their presentation to their students' needs, instruction slows to a more realistic pace, with careful decisions about what material to include and what to save for another day.

Stepping Back From Teaching Style

As a teacher, you accurately identify your own approach as a combination of styles; often you use more than one style on a particular Sunday. Each style evokes different student responses, and some are more compatible with your personality than others. Said one CES instructor, "I lecture because that's the style with which I'm most comfortable and the one in which I'm able to do my best." We each invoke our own best styles which often change over different contexts. I use one style with students in my university classes and a different one with Institute students, *even though the groups are approximately the same age.* The nature of the class, the subject matter and the contexts demand different styles.

Teachers are often counseled to use "a variety of different methods" in their teaching. More important, however, is to select a style, a personal method, *which most expresses your inner self, that part of your teaching which blesses student's lives.* If your inner self surfaces more through tightly-planned lectures, then you do all the talking. If open and easy discussion allows your spiritual nature to best show through, then use discussion. If an eclectic personal style opens your inner self wonderfully to your students, then you will be more effective by invoking it. Your inner self, far more than your method, is the salvation of both you and your students.

Looking Within Styles

Several events and concepts relevant across styles are worth discussing at this point.

Discussion

As classrooms have been videotaped, a surprising characteristic emerges. "Discussion" is primarily a brief exchange between the teacher and a single student, but seldom an exchange among students. Other students cue up for their turn to talk to the teacher. "Discussion," then, is most often comments made to the teacher by a sequence of students. When genuine discussions do arise—students listening to and talking with each other—they are seldom allowed to culminate because the teacher takes back control of the lesson.

Effective discussions reflect the other-centered confidence of the teacher's inner self:

1. Powerful messages give rise to productive discussions.
2. Discussions arise spontaneously without being "drummed up."
3. The teacher feels free to go on "inspired digressions."
4. The teacher centers more on students teaching each other and worries less about loss of control.

The Less Is More Concept

As a Church culture, we are well schooled in sitting through long meetings. Being present in body, however, does not insure sustained attention to even the most scintillating lessons. Our data show that students take mental excursions, fading in and out even when lessons are stimulating and well prepared. And the more packed the lesson, the greater the number of excursions. Again, students have absolute veto power over their attention, regardless of the teacher's level of preparation. Presenting less material with deliberation, depth and detail increases student attention. In preparation and in teaching, "less is more" is a helpful principle.

Spirit-directed Improvisation

We are confronted with a paradox: Teachers are counseled to follow lesson material as outlined, yet some of the most powerful happenings occur during improvisation: a moment when the teacher switches gears, changes directions, engages in unplanned and unanticipated events which bless student lives:

> "I was moving through the lesson and, on the spot, decided to switch and break the class down into pairs to talk about struggles they as teenagers have in keeping the Sabbath."

> "I hadn't prepared for what happened. We were going through several scriptures on the sins of the daughters of Zion, and the class attitude was swelling in a direction uncalled for, so I turned to a different group of scriptures."

"All of a sudden it occurred to me these children needed an opportunity to openly talk about their prayers so I stopped everything, re–arranged the chairs into a circle, and started by sharing my own feelings."

Improvising always takes place on our way to do something else, as we see in the scriptures. Consider two examples:

> Elisha had a habit of passing through Shunem during his prophetic labors and was one day constrained by a Shunammite woman to stay and eat bread. Stopping by this home, taking food, and even finding a bed became a routine for the holy man. Elisha, wanting to repay her kindness, asked, "What is to be done for thee?" Gehazi his servant replied "She hath no child, and her husband is old." He promised her a son. She conceived and bore the son, who one day was injured in an accident and subsequently died. She fled to Elisha for help; he returned and brought the son back to life.[6]

> "He [Jesus] left Judea and departed again into Galilee. And he must needs go through Samaria" and Sychar where Jacob's well is located.[7] Probably tired, hungry and thirsty, he stopped for a drink and was met by a Samarian woman who had come to draw water. Requesting a drink from her, he used this moment to teach her of His "living water" now available to her.[8]

I replay an example from my own teaching. In my Institute class we came one night to 2 Nephi 5: 20-25, where the Lamanites are cursed by being cut off from the presence of the Lord. Then, "that they might not be enticing unto my people the Lord God did cause a skin of blackness to come upon them" to keep the seed from mixing with that of those who had not been cursed. An African American girl, attending for the first time, felt devalued and resentful even though she had participated in the blessings of the temple. Tension filled the room. Well-meaning Caucasian students began citing scriptures of love and inclusion. Courteously enduring through their responses, she expressed, "thanks but no thanks." Her feelings were aroused, and she wanted to express them. Our march toward the concept of "protection through covenant keeping" was insignificant beside this emotional exchange over cultural differences. Almost inadequately, I improvised. Our objective became "empathy rather than reconciliation." I stopped all comments and asked for a moment of silence. Then I asked the African American student, "Would you tell us again your feelings about moving to Utah as a black woman, coming to BYU, experiencing this culture, and going through the temple. Would you help us understand your reactions to these scriptures. We will do our best to listen, to hear your feelings, and to see our culture as you see it." The tension was just bearable- but the change of direction did its work. There was no escape, no reconciliation, only genuine empathy and concern.

A teacher who is in harmony with the gentle promptings of the Spirit, through ongoing study and thoughtful preparation, is able to move in a variety of directions that may be called for during the lesson. Unfortunately, some teachers experience these feelings but set them aside in order to "stay with the lesson." Living closer to the Spirit in daily life and studying the Gospel prayerfully will increase a teacher's confidence in improvising when prompted. Scriptural counsel encourages us to take greater advantage of Spirit-directed improvisation:

> "Neither take ye thought beforehand what ye shall say; but treasure up in your minds continually the words of life, and it shall be given you in the very hour that portion that shall be meted unto every man."[9]

Silence

Silence during our teaching, as during our testimony meetings, can be frightening. When we fail to use silence in our Church teaching, we neglect a powerful force. I quote statements by Parker Palmer, a thoughtful, reflective educator:

> I also use periods of silence in the middle of a class, especially in an open discussion when the words start to tumble out upon each other and the problem we are trying to unravel is getting more tangled. I try to help my

students learn to spot those moments and settle into a time of quiet reflection in which the knots might come untied. We need to abandon the notion that "nothing is happening" when it is silent, to see how much new clarity silence often brings.[10]

In a later book, Palmer continued his consideration of the value of silence:

> But the silences that interest me most are the ones that occur midstream in a discussion, when a point is made or a question is posed that evokes no immediate response.
>
> As the seconds tick by and the silence deepens, my belief in the value of silence goes on trial. Like most people, I am conditioned to interpret silence as a symptom of something gone wrong. I am the ... leader ... so in the silence my sense of competence and worth is at stake: I am the one who must set right what has gone wrong-by speaking. Panic catapults me to the conclusion that the point just made or the question just raised has left the students either dumfounded or bored, and I am duty-bound to apply conversational CPR.
>
> But suppose my panic has misled me and my quick conclusion is mistaken. Suppose that my students are neither dumfounded nor dismissive but digging deep; suppose that they are not ignorant or cynical but wise enough to know that this moment calls for thought; suppose that they are not wasting time but doing a more reflective form of learning. I miss all such possibilities when I assume that their silence signifies a problem, reacting to it from my own need for control rather than their need to learn.
>
> Even if my hopeful interpretations are mistaken, it is indisputable that the moment I break the silence, I foreclose on all chances for authentic learning. Why would my students think their own thoughts in the silence when they know I will invariably fill it with thoughts of my own?[11]

Teacher Questions

Predominant in review teaching, and laced through all other styles, is the technique of teacher questioning. Overwhelmingly, the purpose of teacher questions is to "promote discussion." In the minds of teachers the easiest part of their teaching is to ask questions which range widely in type, specificity and frequency. At the one end of the spectrum are *numbing questions,* those colossal questions whose answers are so self-evident that students are left staring into space:

"Brethren, do any of you ever sin?"

"Who loves children?"

"Has anyone in this room ever been tried and tested?"

"Did the resurrection really happen?"

"Can we be saved?"

"Do married couples ever have differences of opinion?"

Equally frequent are "right answer" or "most appropriate answer" questions found in lesson manuals, generally invoked by teachers during review teaching:

"Who was Leah?"

"Where were the Northern and Southern kingdoms located?"

"What were the sufferings of Job?"

"What is an Elias?"

"What do we need to do to prepare for going through the temple?"

Review questions, whatever the teaching style, are clearly appropriate when the teacher is checking for understanding of a new concept or is reminding students of last week's lesson material.

Less frequent are *reflective* questions, those for which rapid-fire responses are not forthcoming. Students think, ponder, then and offer personal responses:

> "How do you feel about being resurrected with the same personality you now possess?"
>
> "Were you to meet the Prophet Joseph Smith coming down the street, what personal questions might you want to ask him?"
>
> "Is it easier for you to sacrifice or obey? Why?"
>
> "I came away from reading 'Nephi's Lament' with personal hope. What were your reactions?"

Teachers might well ask themselves, "For what purpose am I asking this question?" Honest responses will cause some to be dropped and others to be revised. Predictably, *fewer* will be asked, and those remaining will evoke greater personal thought among students.

In their packed lessons, teachers find it difficult to wait, to pause quietly as students process thought-provoking questions. Research shows the average wait time is less than three seconds! This same research shows that as teachers wait (up to 15-20) seconds, quality of student responses improves, more students participate, and many other good things happen. Then good things continue as the teacher waits after a student responds before offering her response. However, if the teacher cannot afford wait time, asking reflective questions does more harm than good: "You ask us to think about the question you pose, but then you go on before we can think about it—was it not important?"

Student Questions And Comments

Few things strike more fear into the heart of an inexperienced teacher than questions and comments from the group; even the hardened veteran can become wary—anticipating a challenge to his or her competence. Other teachers, however, are energized by active student involvement, unafraid of mistakes, lapses or correction.

An unwritten contract should exist between teacher and student: I and the rest of the class welcome your questions and comments; in turn I will treat them with care and respect. This contract is violated when the teacher offers a passing "Thank you for your comment" then hurriedly moves on. Our interview data suggest that students often feel put off or devalued because their comments receive no response—as if student responses are not really part of the lesson but an activity tolerated by the teacher as part of classroom etiquette. "Throwing Justin's question back to the class" helps neither Justin nor the class. Respectfulness includes careful listening, focused thinking, and thoughtful response *before* asking others for additions or corrections.

Individual student voices braided into a larger group voice is the goal of every good teacher. Gathering student comments and questions and focusing them around the subject is a skill both teacher and students need to learn: "Bryce, show us how your comment relates to what Heather just said"; "Students, use your comments to instruct us further on today's subject"; "I will try to relate your comments to the subject but will need your help."

My classroom observations suggest that relevant student questions and comments flow naturally from thoughtful messages: The more thought invested in the message, the more thought will be reflected in student responses. Good messages do not require additional tactics in order to generate involvement. Students overflow with questions—and introspection—when messages are well prepared.

Often students do not wish for quick fixes from the teacher; they simply want to be heard; and equally as often, they already have an answer for their question. With discernment and sensitivity the teacher responds, "Don't you already have an answer to your question? If you have thought about this issue, would you be willing to share your thinking with us?"

Finally, Elder Neal A. Maxwell's advice is worth noting: "Don't answer questions students are not asking." A corollary is if students come for a drink don't turn on the fire hydrant.

<u>With-it-ness</u>

High school students, when interviewed about their teachers, conjure up colorful descriptors:

"The lights are on but nobody's home."

"His elevator doesn't go to the top floor."

"She hasn't the foggiest idea what's going on."

"She has smarts!"

"Man, he is with it."

When the last respondent was asked about being "with it," an equally interesting description came forth:

> "It's like he has a wire going from every kid to his head so he knows what's going on every minute. He turns to write on the board and he can tell you who will be talking and who's passing notes. The minute he explains something, he knows who has understood, who needs help, and who will never get it."

Junior high and high school teachers called to teach in Young Women or the Aaronic Priesthood tend to be unusually effective, partly because they are experienced professional teachers, but mostly because they have developed *instincts* for teaching youth. They know the developmental stages of teenagers, their peer group pressures, their needs, their motivations, their fears and insecurities, their ways of calling out for attention and acceptance, their ways of thinking, and the conditions under which they best learn. They know the leaders, the followers, the fringies, the stoners, the skaters, the Gothics; who is going steady, who has a crush on whom, who are the college bound, and who are at high risk.

Aside from so-called "natural" gifts, any teacher can develop teaching instincts, including *with-it-ness*. Any teacher can get inside the heads and hearts of students: come to understand how to promote their best learning; how to pace lesson instruction; how to find examples, stories and scriptures that permit them to "connect" with the lesson material. Any teacher can develop a sense for making the message relevant to his or her particular class and for presenting it in an interesting and digestible form.

Teacher Expectations

Master elementary teachers engage in *grooving* during the first few weeks of school. The curriculum becomes "how we go to school in my classroom," which includes where to hang coats and store lunches, how to get excused to use the bathroom and wash hands, how to respect the private space of each person's desk or table area, what to do or not to do at the teacher's desk, when to sharpen pencils, how to store playground equipment and a host of other procedures. Effective teachers, says the research, are very good at establishing routines.

Grooving is simply the process of establishing expectations. Any time a Church teacher enters a classroom, he or she sets expectations, most of the time unknowingly. How powerful and how under exploited! Teachers mourn "too many irrelevant comments" or "the same few do all the talking," but observation of their classes reveals that they expect—and therefore reinforce—these student behaviors. In contrast, the teacher of the eight-year-olds may come in with the expectation "I don't have time for disruptive behavior and neither do you." Her treatment of the students reveals this expectation and, sure enough, students contribute to her self-fulfilling prophecy.

Expectations are announced through the total behavior of the teacher rather than by a set of verbal statements. Your dress, your classroom demeanor, your organization, and your teaching style all express your inner self and reveal your expectations to your students. Here is a sample of expectations felt by students:

Success is brewing!

Our class will be friendly, and we will move ahead.

Important ideas are going to be born in this classroom.

You will soon realize the importance of having your scriptures with you.

Time is important.

Comments are invited, but make them relevant.

You will not want to monopolize the time—you will, however, want to contribute with the rest of the class members.

This is a safe environment.

We are going to be wonderfully accepting of all comments.

In this class we will focus on the spiritual.

Our lessons will be Christ centered.

Regularly, the difference between productive and listless classes can be found in the types of expectations teachers set. This is an exciting concept, well worth study in one's own teaching.

Manipulation of Emotions

Urgent teaching and preaching are characterized by manipulation of student emotions and feelings in order to achieve a teacher's ends. Teachers of youth and teenagers, especially, may find it difficult to resist acting on tender vulnerabilities with such topics as moral purity and drug-free living. Our interviews with students suggest that the distinction between emotionalism and the Spirit become blurred when teachers attempt to manipulate feelings for what they hope will be good results. Following are reflections about manipulation:

"Some of my most emotional childhood experiences were watching Church videos. They seemed to be calculated to make you cry. As youth, we all knew this and expected it. Usually someone would die in the video: a little boy's mom, an old lady who never got mail, or an old painter who stayed up all night to paint a leaf in the alley. Our youth leaders would wheel the TV and VCR tray into our classroom . . . . We knew exactly what to expect. Usually we had seen the movie several times before, and cried each time. We never like it when we cried, but we just couldn't help it . . . . When the moment came that Bobby's mom had to go, it was always the girls that started with the sniffling. The teacher had tissues ready.

Then the guys would start to go. We would try hard to fight it. It just wasn't cool for a teenager to cry. I would bite my cheek and look down on the ground as if I were tired . . . . When the movie was over and the lights were up, the teacher, sometimes wiping the tears from her own eyes, looked upon the class of red eyes and sniffling noses and asked us for our feelings on the video. The girls would usually say something like 'I'm going to write a letter to my grandmother as soon as I get home.' The guys, less likely to get the point of the movie, and unwilling to give the teacher any gratification, would say things like 'If only the kid had taken the poster instead of the fish bowl, he wouldn't have gotten hit by the car'."

"There is a great conflict in the Church today regarding sentimentalism and true spiritual experiences. People are bringing in more and more stories and music meant to manipulate our emotions. Growing up in the Church, I have heard countless stories [for example, the returning missionary in his tattered suit in a relieving sleep with his worn scriptures opened on his lap]. I have to admit, I love stories like this one. However, it's primary purpose, and that for which it was read to us, is to evoke emotion and draw a tear. I am very vulnerable to this kind of emotional manipulation. It is a huge part of learning in the Seminary and Sunday School programs of the Church. Growing up, kids are often deceived into thinking that a sentimental surge, a story that tugs at the heartstrings, is a genuine spiritual experience."

"[My teacher] is a very emotional man, but in this particular case, I felt like he trespassed beyond what was naturally acceptable to teach. We were having a special program to learn more about the sacrament. The students and the teachers all gathered in the upper auditorium of the Jerusalem Center where a fully garnished triclenium decorated the stage. Some of the students had volunteered to re-enact 'The Last Supper' according to Roman traditions. After the demonstration, this teacher talked about Jesus and His life on the earth. It was a wonderful teaching setting and the information was good, but the teacher started to manipulate our emotions when he began to extend the truth. Most of us had already read the life of Christ in the New Testament or from conference talks. It is a familiar subject, but this teacher started to include details that no one has heard of, which no one could have possibly documented. He said that Christ grew up as a very poor boy, probably scrawny and malnourished with dark circles under his eyes. I had never pictured Christ this way, hence I felt violated when the teacher thrust these emotional details on me when they were not warranted. I left feeling disturbed and uneasy."

"Yes, I have felt manipulated in Relief Society, mostly due to a common preconception in the Church, which is that feeling the Spirit means that you cry. I've gotten the impression that many Relief Society teachers equate their teaching success with how many sniffles they hear and how many people are wiping their eyes—this impression comes because these teachers constantly tell stories and personal experiences that seem more emotional in nature than instructional, and they encourage members of the class to do the same. While these stories may strike an emotional chord in me, I'm never quite sure that I'm learning anything, nor am I sure that I'm feeling the Spirit."

"We teach so that students can make better decisions in life based on the knowledge that they have acquired within themselves. If we teach by manipulating our students' emotions, we deprive them from seeing the truth about life and inhibit their ability to make rational decisions, and as a result, we violate the very sacred charge with which we have been entrusted, to teach."

Teachers can feel comfortable in the assurance that the Gospel message will do its own work. There is no need for unnatural emphasis, over teaching, insistence, garnishing or, as President Packer says, "making the Gospel truer than it is."[12] Stated in a slightly different way by Elder Jeffrey R. Holland, "Work at being balanced and steady; don't push the sensational or the extreme; be sensible when there is something you don't know."[13]

Humor

Like expectations, humor be powerful in sacred Gospel teaching. It unplugs tension, relieves fatigue and boredom, and heals wounded feelings. But most of all, it provides perspective when either teachers or students take themselves too seriously or exaggerate their own importance.

Jokes, being humor on demand, are superficial in the relief they provide, and they may come across as irreverent. The spattered laughter is strained and superficially accommodating. Everyone is ready to move on. But spontaneous laughter which arises from the lesson or from acknowledging our human condition is wonderfully rewarding. Unplanned, unpredictable, often escalating, never-to-be repeated, it bonds the group warmly and refreshingly.

Visual Aids

Upon entering a fifth-grade class in Palo Alto, I was immediately confronted by an imposing covered wagon. Two "pioneers" were putting finishing touches on their wooden rifles.

"What are you doing?"

"Making guns!"

The enthusiastic teacher hurried to greet us, dressed in her long dress and bonnet.

"What is happening in this bee hive of activity?"

"We're studying pioneer life; I want kids to get it first hand."

Visual aids can be so exaggerated that they become ends in and of themselves. And this exaggeration is not necessarily limited to classes of young children. While serving in a BYU campus ward, I was invited to attend Relief Society, which was at that time held on the first floor of the Jesse Knight Humanities Building. As this floor is underground, closing the door thrusts the occupants into total darkness. On this particular Sunday, all the sisters and I sat in this darkness waiting for the lesson to begin. Suddenly a kaleidoscope was turned on. We gasped, thinking we had mistakenly entered an amusement park. Lining the walls on all four sides of the room were 26 full-length mirrors, reflecting the rotating colored lights—a breathtaking spectacle! I shall never be able to reconstruct the message given that day, but the thrilling display of mirrors is forever stamped in my memory. In the apartment complex for which I was responsible as Bishop, 26 mirrors had been removed from the same number of apartments—a several night effort. Obviously, no time had been left to prepare the lesson, which should have been titled "The Moving of Mirrors."

Visual aids are, as the term states, aids to understanding the message. They should enhance rather than detract from or replace the message. Always simple, they are concrete instances of the concept being taught, or they serve as images to trigger meaning or ideas previously learned. They carry meaning that can apply to scriptural stories or events. For example, on a trip to Guatemala we climbed temples, went onto lakes, stopped at mountains, overlooked land masses, visited artifacts—all to illustrate for us what life and conditions might have been like at the time of the Nephites and Lamanites. These concrete examples helped us create mental images which can be called up when reading The Book of Mormon. Having been "on site" compels a person to read The Book of Mormon differently than had the trip not been made.

Loving arrangements of plants on tables covered with matching table cloths, pictures tastefully displayed, floral presentations and conducive music are adornments to create a spirit of refinement and worship. Their role is to create an atmosphere while visual aids are to facilitate understanding of the message.

Standing Back

As you come to greater awareness of what is taking place in Church classrooms, the different ways teachers' inner selves are expressed through public teaching become readily apparent. The different styles of teaching and the different aspects within styles tend to reveal the nature of the inner self that drives and permeates the flow of the lesson. Reflecting upon this dynamic interaction between a person's inner self and her teaching, we have traveled through this teaching terrain.

Further, we see that if styles and classroom activities are to change, the inner self must change, especially as repentance purifies the individual's motives and concerns.

[1] Alma 36:2.
[2] Alma 36:29.
[3] 1 Nephi 14:8.
[4] Elder Neal A. Maxwell, CES Fireside, February 20, 2000.
[5] 1 Nephi 19:23.
[6] 2 Kings 4: 8–37.
[7] "His smallest choices were always filled with meaning." *The Source of the Light.*
[8] 1 John 4: 1–30.
[9] Doctrine and Covenants 84:84.
[10] Parker J. Palmer. *To Know As We Are Known.* San Francisco: Harper, 1983, p. 82.
[11] Parker J. Palmer. *The Courage To Teach.* San Francisco: Jossey-Bass, 1998, p. 82. Copyright 1998 by Jossey-Bass Inc. Publishers. Reprinted by permission of Jossey-Bass Inc., A subsidiary of John Wiley & Sons, Inc.
[12] Talk at a stake leadership meeting, Provo, Utah, about 1995.
[13] Talk at a CES fireside, Salt Lake City, Utah, 1999.

CHAPTER 6

TEACHER BELIEFS

"Personal predispositions are not only relevant but, in fact, stand at the core of becoming a teacher."[1]

Plodding and Boring

Several years ago, while studying the teaching practices of Seminary teachers, I stumbled onto a powerful phenomenon. In partnership with several colleagues in the School of Technology, I had developed a computer system capable of unobtrusively gathering information from students while they were being taught. We placed a small 2"X 4"pad on each student's desk, hooked to a wire running to a computer at the back of the room. On the pad were three words: "Attending?" "Interested?" "Understanding?" Above each was a small light-emitting diode which could be lit up with the press of a computer key. Also on the pad were five buttons with the following words above them: "Yes!" "Yes" "Somewhat" "No" "No!" A small wire ran from the pad to an earpiece fitted into the student's ear. Every few minutes, from our computer in the back of the room we "beeped" the class through their earpieces to signal them to look down at their pad. If the small light came on over "Attending?" (or "Interested?" or "Understanding?") the student hit the button best describing his or her state of mind at that moment: "Yes!" "Yes" "Somewhat" "No" or "No!" After several "beeps," students became accustomed to their task, and it was no longer intrusive for them. After each response, the computer instantly displayed response patterns of the class in the form of bar graphs. Concurrently the teacher's talking was being recorded on videotape, thus enabling us to synchronize how the class was responding at each point in the lesson. This procedure allowed us to quietly communicate with students *as they were being taught.*

Brother E. allowed us to set up our computer system in his room to work out the bugs before seriously gathering data. Coincidentally, we had been videotaping his teaching over several weeks on another project. Each day five classes of 25-30 students participated in this procedure. During any given class period students were "beeped" an average of 18 times. By the end of five days we had gathered a mountain of student responses!

As part of another project, we had Brother E. view videotapes of his classes, which confirmed to him his long-held perception that he was "a plodding and boring teacher." His wife, who occasionally visited his classes, affirmed this belief: "Honey, you're a good man and a righteous example to these kids—but you're not the most exciting teacher in the world." After the classroom visit, his supervisor quipped, "Are you sure you don't want to go into administration?" Brother E. had come to accept the view of his wife and his supervisor that he was plodding and boring as a teacher—but a good person.

What happened next was an unanticipated surprise. We placed before him the summaries of these student responses. While students did not see him as charismatic or as the most interesting Seminary teacher they had ever had, they did *not* see him as boring! Brother E. studied the data in disbelief. He insisted on taking them home to show his wife. Still her view remained unchanged: "You know I love you and to me you are everything I have ever hoped for—but no matter what the kids say, you are not their most exciting Seminary teacher. You have other compensating qualities."

Several days later he came striding into our research room. "You know what? I've decided to believe these kids. They can't all be wrong. Maybe I'm the one who is wrong. Maybe my wife is wrong." We immediately started the camera rolling again. Within two or three days, Brother E. was acting like a different person! He showed new confidence, handled misbehavior with firmness, told jokes, spoke with greater authority and started relating to the students in surprising ways. We grabbed students coming out his classes. Some were puzzled: "What's happened to this guy?" "He's all of a sudden different." "I don't know what it is, but he's changed."

Serendipitously, we had arrived at an important understanding: A person's beliefs about himself powerfully affect the way he teaches. When those beliefs change, so also does his teaching. We pursued this finding in later studies and came to an additional conclusion: A person's teaching does not permanently change until his or her beliefs change—beliefs circumscribe classroom behavior. For example, we encouraged a Seminary teacher who saw himself as humorless to tell jokes and try to be funny. His attempts were a dismal failure.

Our results have been confirmed by a growing body of research on teachers' thinking and their personal theories: personal beliefs pervasively influence how teachers teach. Here are examples of personal beliefs from our observations and interviews with Church teachers. You might think about how they would sway that person's teaching:

> "My role is to prepare and present lessons."
> "I do an adequate job but I always want to improve."
> "I can't teach without the Spirit."
> "Teaching is presenting lessons."
> "You learn to teach by jumping in and teaching."
> "I don't get much out of in-service lessons."
> "Anyone can become a good teacher if they work at it."
> "Some people are just born good teachers."
> "I should try to teach like the Savior taught."
> "There is such a thing as an ideal teacher."
> "Everything in the lesson should be covered if at all possible."
> "You improve by preparing better."
> "Lesson objectives may be important but I don't use to them."
> "Asking questions is a good way to get the class involved."
> "Teachers should not lecture; students need to get involved in discussions."
> "Good discussions are the best measure of your success."
> "Relating to your class is critical."
> "If I had more time to prepare I'd do a better job.'
> "I'm really the only one who can improve my teaching."
> "I gauge my success by how well the lesson went."
> "These are spirit children of our Heavenly Father."
> "Sharing personal experiences is very important."
> "Some days I make no difference at all!"

Recognizing the Need

Several years ago I offered a faculty workshop in "Test Construction" at the university. One department chair had urged all members of his department to attend; about 25% showed up. He asked me to inquire of the non–attendees why they had chosen not to attend. Overwhelmingly, the response was "I don't see the need; I've been making good tests for years." Some indeed were good test constructors, but most had a history of student complaints about hopelessly invalid exams. The private theories of these faculty that they constructed good tests actually prevented them from improving their exams.

The same has happened when Church teachers have been interviewed about non–attendance at teacher development meetings: "The things I hear will not help me that much in my teaching. The leader will try to motivate me to be a good teacher, but I'm already motivated and I am a good teacher." Attendance will not improve until teachers change their private theories about themselves as teachers.

Does daily repentance alter a teacher's personal beliefs? Sometimes. If faculty humble themselves before students, they "hear" those complaints which are legitimate and respond with better tests. They become sensitive to all aspects of their teaching. Adversarial relationships are replaced by compassionate relationships where teachers see ever more clearly the needs and responses of those in their charge. But there are some humble teachers who are simply naive, who are simply unaware of what personal theories they hold and how their teaching is influenced by their theories. They are awakened and respond quickly as their study creates new awarenesses.

Examining Our Personal Beliefs

Since our beliefs about teaching—whether deeply hidden or readily accessible—do influence our practice, to unearth and examine them is a worthwhile activity. Some are worth holding on to, while others need replacing, updating, and revising. Inaccurate and unproductive beliefs tend to impede a teacher's continuing development, while powerful beliefs free up the log jam.

One approach is to study your teaching behavior then infer the beliefs reflected in it. Several examples will help:

Over a 40-minute class period you "throw out" a lot of questions, 28 to be exact. For example: What do we know about Laman and Lemuel? Who was the leader and who was the follower? How did father Lehi treat them? Why was the family required to wander for eight years in the wilderness? How did Nephi respond when the Lord instructed him to build a ship? What was Laman and Lemuel's reaction? Responses to the questions are volunteered by different members of the class. Looking back on the lesson, you ask yourself, "What do I believe about the use of questions in teaching?" You might respond, "Students feel involved when they have a chance to participate by answering questions—and involvement is important."

Consider another example. You continually use concrete objects in your teaching: a menorah, pottery, oil lamps, smooth stones, an apple, a top, jello, flute, fiber from a rope, coins. They become metaphors: Our lives can become these smooth stones; one cannot describe the feelings of the Spirit any more than the taste of an apple; we need to have oil in our spiritual lamps; we may worship idols in our lives. Stepping back you ask yourself, "Why do I use objects in my teaching?" You might answer, "Students have direct experience with objects in the physical world and can easily relate to them in dealing with abstract concepts (e.g. endurance, spirituality, cooperation, internal strength, readiness)."

Let's look at another example: In teaching Beehives you notice you often bring in treats and repeatedly ask the girls' indulgence as you present your lessons. You find ways to compliment each girl, plan activities for the group in your home during the week (baking cookies, making gifts for widows), and sit with them during sacrament meetings. You serve as counselor and mother surrogate whenever possible. Stepping back, you ask yourself, "What do I believe about how testimonies are built in young women?" You might reflect, "Girls at this age need models to imitate, models who love them, who are their friends. They need models even more than lessons."

We consider one final example: You study the manner in which you prepare lessons. First you read the lesson (or scriptural chapters) over several times. You go back into the scriptures reading the context for each and do some cross referencing for additional possibilities. You start out with an outline which quickly emerges into a detailed lesson with phrases, stories and scriptures all written out. You agonize over the sequence, also deciding what needs to be omitted, because by now you have over packed the lesson. You retype the lesson, then begin the rehearsal stage where, behind closed doors with clock in view, you go over and over it until a polished presentation flows almost from memory. Daily until Sunday morning, you continue reworking sections, inserting a statement you just read from the Brethren or a scripture you just discovered on the topic. You have developed a finished lesson which is not finished. Going into the meetings, your stress increases as you realize that you have prepared an hour's worth of material to be covered within 35 minutes. Stepping back, you ask yourself, "What do I believe is my role as teacher?" You might respond, "To present the best possible lessons," or "Students learn best from teachers who have a deep understanding of the material and are able to present it in clear and interesting ways."

Another approach to discovering your personal beliefs is through metaphors. As an exercise, I ask my students to come up with metaphors which describe them as teachers: "A teacher is a . . . ." Interesting images arise: gardener, coach, symphony conductor, policeman, tour guide, mother hen, drill sargent, hard-hat supervisor, sky-diving instructor, puppet master, magician, sculptor, scoutmaster, farmer who plants and irrigates. How easy it is for a girl from a family of ten, veteran of unnumbered baby sitting experiences, to describe a teacher's role as mother hen. Or a young man who has been an eagle scout and worked on a boy's ranch might see his teaching role as that of a tour guide (or a drill sargent!).

I ask students to describe their metaphors in detail, picturing themselves as actual classroom teachers. One student identified herself as a potter: "I throw a formless piece of clay on my wheel and begin shaping my students—their minds and souls—into decent, informed, law-abiding citizens. I play a major role in deciding on the image and its form as I mold and shape lives and help create testimonies." Another explained: "As a midwife I help usher out what is already there and partially formed. In the birthing of ideas and testimony, I set the environment, facilitate, lend support, step in now and then in bringing ideas, understandings and testimonies to fruition."

Creating and expanding your teaching metaphor reveals your beliefs about teaching. Changing over time and with experience, these metaphors will mirror your maturing beliefs about teaching which, in turn, modify your teaching behavior. Use them.

Recognizing Our Toe-Stubbing Beliefs

Some beliefs are incompletely formed, partly accurate; others are short sighted, restrictive and even inaccurate. Such beliefs cause stumbling and often divert the teacher from his or her primary responsibility of inviting students to Christ. Here is a sample:

<u>"My responsibility is to prepare and present lessons."</u>
True, the teacher is responsible for careful preparation and organized presentation. But if this belief is predominant, a teacher may allow the means to become the end. Building testimonies, inviting people to Christ, and encouraging a higher plane of living should be the ends to which preparing and presenting are directed. "Obviously," responds the onlooker, "We all have that in the back of our minds each Sunday." However, a teacher's preoccupation with tightly-developed outlines crammed with special stories, scriptures, and quotes takes on a life of its own, with a focus on the lesson itself rather than on the students. And, sadly, this focus does not often shift to student needs, concerns, and testimonies. With such a change in focus, polished lessons would give way to (or be revised to include) teaching which benefits the students. But when students realize that the teacher's central goal is to move efficiently through the lesson and cover the material before the second bell rings, they check out in various ways: meandering through their scriptures, carrying on private conversations, passing notes, going to sleep, leaving before class is over.

<u>"Ones size fits all."</u>
The curriculum for Melchizedek Priesthood and Relief Society may be more standardized now than at any other time in Church history. In an effort to promote Gospel discussion between husbands and wives, both groups now use the same manual. This curricular consolidation has reinforced a belief that is already widespread among teachers: that one size fits all, that a given lesson can (and should) be presented in the same way in every setting. The Brethren do not

intend this standardization. Actually, talks and written materials urge teachers to prayerfully consider the uniqueness of their own setting and to adapt each lesson to meet the needs of their learners.

If there is a single pervasive weakness in Church teaching, it is the surprising inattention of teachers to the needs of those whom they teach. This weakness flows from the belief that the teacher's role is to present lessons. Preoccupied and busy with "preparing what's in the manual," the teacher feels that her responsibility has been fulfilled: "I work hard to do my part, to get this material ready; if students fail to partake, I feel badly but I've done all I'm supposed to do." Quite innocently, teachers ignore the contexts in which they teach, expecting students to make adjustments to receive the lesson as written. This can be observed throughout the ward: the Relief Society teacher talking about marital harmony when half the sisters are either single or divorced; the high priest instructor trying to persuade a group of former bishops and stake presidents there was in fact an apostasy; the Laurel teacher talking about the importance of dieting when two of the five girls are suffering from eating disorders; the Seminary teacher treating her adult Sunday School class like her early morning Seminary; and the teachers quorum advisor using the same strategies to relate to African American teachers in Nashville, Tennessee that he did with Caucasian teachers in Provo, Utah. But there is comic relief. The average age of men in our high priest group is near 70. All have been married at least 30 years, have reared children, and are puffed up about their growing progenies. One priesthood lesson, forbearingly endured, was titled "The Importance of the Family." Without blinking an eye (or placing tongue in cheek), our instructor walked dutifully through the lesson, firmly cautioning us not to put off having children until we were financially secure—only 50 years too late.

"Cover everything in the lesson manual."

This belief spins off from the concept "teaching equals presenting" and "one size fits all." To cover the manual requires the teacher to either blaze through an overload of thoroughly prepared material, leaving the students reeling, or "merely touch upon" a wide range of topics. Students have no choice but to support the teacher on his quest by refraining from questions or comments. The class becomes teacher centered rather than student centered.

"To be really effective you have to have been professionally trained."

More often than not this toe-stubbing belief is offered to justify mediocrity, a result of an unwillingness to pay the price: "Not being a professional teacher, I'm not expected to be more than average; after all, I didn't volunteer for this calling." True, professional teachers have learned through preparation and experience about presenting concepts creatively, pacing the lesson appropriately, adapting to student needs, judging how much material is realistic for a given unit of time, teaching to individual differences, providing rewards and managing classrooms, and dealing with disruptive behavior. But many untrained teachers are blessed with a seemingly innate ability to connect with students, to draw them out, to explain concepts in clear and meaningful ways; having what high school students call "with-it-ness." With effort, each of us can become the best teacher that is in us to be—but few of us reach *that* potential. Students reciprocate with their own mediocrity, matching the teacher's level of seriousness and commitment with their own.

"I want to become *the* ideal teacher."

Though an admirable goal, this orientation may leave a teacher frustrated and discouraged. When interviewed, teachers will often say, "My ideal is the Savior. I want to teach like He did." We all have that desire. The challenge is to live a life similar enough to His life to merit being able to teach as He taught. But the disparity is so great we often become discouraged. We find ourselves, for example, aspiring to His compassion while succumbing to natural-man emotions, and we may give up. As we struggle enroute to perfection, we conjure up an earthly model with all the desired traits: "An ideal teacher is loving, patient, able to respond to the individual needs of each student, full of knowledge about the subject, clear and understandable, humble and so forth."

We are instructed by our leaders to teach like the Savior taught. Many have reached a level of sanctification which allows them to exhibit Christlike characteristics in their teaching. In pursuing perfection we must *first* become the best teacher that is in us to be, looking inward first, then upward to a higher model. Our own best teaching self should be our preliminary model, a goal more possible to attain, less likely to lead to frustration. We might ask, "What does my teaching look like when I'm the best teacher I can be?" Discouragement can lead to fabrication: "While not reaching the ideal, I can at least imitate the Savior's techniques in my teaching." Students, especially teenagers, turn away when they think they see duplicity in their teacher.

"The best way to improve is to spend more time preparing."
This is a partially accurate belief. Few would deny the importance of preparation; indeed, deep preparation is as critical as any other single factor in successful teaching. However, this belief causes teachers to concentrate on only one dimension for improvement, preparing lesson material. The underlying message of this book is that growth results from working along a number of dimensions: the perfecting inner self, developing positive relationships, transforming one's knowledge into teaching knowledge, being sensitive to the context, and so forth. A polished presentation, reflecting hours of thoughtful work, may fall on deaf ears if the teacher is not able to connect with her students. Likewise, no amount of serious Gospel scholarship can compensate for lack of clarity in communicating with students.

"Discussions will involve students in the lesson."
This is also a partially accurate belief. All of us have experience which confirms the importance of involvement and the efficacy of productive discussions. Too often, however, "involvement" is considered synonymous with getting people to talk. True, some students can think while talking—but reflecting, resolving, committing and repenting occur in silence, as private internal work. When I have interviewed students, I have found that a surprising number do not "feel involved" when asking a question or volunteering a comment. A thought or opinion comes to them, and they decide to voice it; having done so, they shift their thoughts to something like "Should I have turned the roast on before I left for Church?" Some students offer comments because "it's the thing to do" or "I just wanted to keep things moving." Of course, others are earnest and thoughtful about their questions and comments. In general, however, discussions do not insure "involvement." And a litany of questions from the teacher or a few minutes of "playing the Devil's advocate" seldom produce serious student involvement. Elder Maxwell has labeled some of these activities as "intellectual ping pong." Unfortu-

nately an overconfidence in the value of discussion causes well-meaning teachers to engage in superficial games with students and invites students to respond with superficial involvement—both going through the motions.

Finally, my research suggests that what we call "discussions" is more accurately a series of solo comments made to the teacher. Students line up for their turn to have a brief interchange with the teacher. Only infrequently does one observe students talking to each other across the room during a "discussion." When genuine communication does occur, the teacher retrieves control with "these are interesting comments but we need to get back on the lesson." (What is this teacher's metaphor?)

"You shouldn't just stand up there and lecture."

Historically, "lecturing" in church classrooms has been the wretched task of reading from the lesson manual, reading one's carefully developed notes, or simply talking at people—any and all of which are boring to students. This toe-stubbing belief causes us to misidentify the culprit, which is the quality of the message, not the mode of its presentation. Good "lecturers" hold teenagers spellbound for periods of two hours during Education Week at BYU; the same is true with countless adult classes. And the same is true with the lecture of any good teacher, regardless of the setting, anywhere in the Church. Misguided in thinking, a teacher—"not wanting to lecture the whole time"—reverts to throwing out a litany of questions surrounding an inadequately conceived message, an approach which can be every bit as boring. This belief diverts the teacher to begin tinkering with method, a desperation measure which does not address the real problem. A rather different belief would be more productive: Any number of methods will be effective if the message is well-conceived.

From this sample of toe-stubbing beliefs, we glimpse how a teacher can become side-tracked and at times imprisoned by personal theories—detained on plateaus of mediocrity. Our task is to critically examine these beliefs and to modify or replace those which impede us.

Adopting Enabling Beliefs

Replacement beliefs can release our potential and maximize our progress.

"Every teacher is unique."

On his popular children's program, Fred Rogers proclaims, "There is nobody else like you." If you apply this belief to your teaching, you turn inward, focusing on the development of your own unique combination of traits. Rather than coveting the relaxed style of Sister Markham, the clarity of Sister Eskelson, the humility of Brother Jensen, the wit of Brother Hawkins, the scriptural scholarship of Sister Randall, you set about enhancing your own endowment: your gentle spirit, your predisposition for detail, your subtle humor, your cautious approach to people, your abject honesty, your intolerance for shoddiness, your emotional nature. It is this unique combination of traits that will ultimately develop the more effective you.

Admiring and attempting to emulate a characteristic from a splendid teacher is a healthy complement to exploration of your personal strengths. These admired and imitated traits are filtered through your own unique self. If you witness effective humor in a valued teacher, you may want to adopt humor in your own teaching. But it must be your unique expression of humor—perhaps subtle rather than boisterous. The valued traits of other teachers must be played on your own piano with your own interpretation. Your students will be most influenced by your uniqueness, not by your imitation of others.

"Teaching always occurs in a particular context."

Too often we consider and address issues in teaching independent of context. Our Church teaching culture is replete with unqualified generalizations: "Always use variety in your teaching," "Always give a challenge at the end of a lesson," "Have students participate in the reading of scriptures," "Videos help to provide variety and relief." But whenever we teach it is *always* within a given context. A successful activity in one context may be awkward in another. For example, a Church video shown to 16 year-olds may be emotionally gripping, while any video shown to a class of seasoned saints may detract from their desire to focus on the scriptures.

Context is the complex interaction of all the factors relevant in a given teaching episode—with you, the teacher, in the middle of it all. First you must consider your students: their characteristics and personalities, backgrounds, maturity levels, needs, interests, and testimonies. Then you look at the nature of the class you are teaching: Beehive, Scouts, Primary, 10 year-olds in Primary, Gospel Essentials, Gospel Doctrine, Relief Society. Physical surroundings are also relevant: room size, ventilation, temperature. Look also at the culture and socio-economic levels of the members and their vocations (or interests), along with their commitments, attitudes, ethnic diversity, and the community in which they live. You take all aspects of the context into account and work with this knowledge in order to bless the lives of your students.

I currently teach in our Stake Institute Program, meeting with 18-30 year-olds each Wednesday night studying, this year, the Book of Mormon. Some in this group work full time, others attend BYU or Utah Valley State College, others neither work nor go to school. For the Institute class, neither college credit nor grades nor weekly reading assignments are important to their participation. They come when they want to and do not show up when they prefer being somewhere else. Refreshments are welcomed after each meeting, but a class party is incidental to spiritual food. We have chosen to ignore semester deadlines and summer breaks and to go each Wednesday year round. Our pace is leisurely, and we explore in depth the Gospel's concepts, peoples' lives, and the Lord's purposes. In one session we may cover two chapters or two verses, always welcoming inspired digressions.

Were I teaching this same Book of Mormon class at BYU, the context would be strikingly different, *though the two groups are within three miles of each other*. At BYU the students are more homogeneous in age, interests, lifestyle, immediate goals, and educational levels. Because they are taking classes for credit, assignments, grades, and regular attendance are necessary in this context. Students in the Institute class are obedient to their own goals—which on a particular night might consist of escaping the grind of their lives. At BYU, my pace would be faster, digressions less frequent, and course mechanics more important.

If a teacher realized the power of context and understood its impact on her influence on her students, she would attend to their lives, their backgrounds, their belief and value systems, their testimonies, and their experiences in and out of the Church. Her lessons would pliably accommodate the demands of this context, to the relief and progress of her students.

"A teacher's influence is inevitable."

How easy to conclude at the end of a frustrating lesson that you might as well have stayed home—or that Josh and Mallory might *better* have stayed at home! Your prodigious preparations, delivered with the urgency of Lehi, have fallen on the deaf ears of ungrateful teenagers. Or, filled with fascinating information, your fast-paced lesson has totally missed your lethargic class of adults. Or you might as well have given your scouts food, knots to tie, and a video—they don't need you. Church teachers hardly lack opportunities for discouragement. The following comment summarizes what many of us feel: "I work *so* hard to prepare and feel lucky if one idea sinks in."

But consider adopting an alternative belief: Everything you say or do has an effect on your students; however modest or inconspicuous, this effect either points to or away from Christ. You cannot prevent yourself from influencing your students. A look, a gesture, a word, the feeling you exude, a comment in the lesson—all produce a cumulative effect upon your students, non–measurable at any given moment. Every small effort you expend is registered on the minds and souls of your students. The reverse is also true. The boring teacher, showing up week after week with only a modicum of preparation, is having a negative effect on students.

As teachers we are intentional: We strive (or hope) to bring about changes in students, changes which move them toward happiness. Simplistically stated, that is what teachers do. But teaching is not simplistic; it is incredibly complex and full of *unintended effects*. We want students to respond to our lessons, but they end up responding to us—who we are as humans and what we represent to them. These unintended effects can damage or build, break or repair. We shrink from this much capriciousness. We want some effects and not others. We want to remove risk as we intrude, often uninvited, into the lives of our students. Sometimes the unintended effect—the "hidden curriculum"—produces stronger results than do our best intentions.

However, we can assume the optimistic alternative: A teacher's influence is inevitable and can be overwhelmingly positive. As a teacher, you have been called by a Priesthood leader, inspired through the Spirit. Your setting apart offers comfort along with authority to receive spiritual promptings. Your righteous intent, coupled with vigorous preparation, opens the way for the Lord to work through you for the good of your students. Every Sunday, then, despite apathy, disruption, and apparent inattention, your time and energy are well spent. Value for your students, though difficult to discern, comes from *every* lesson. Students feel your assurance of this influence, your unwavering commitment, and they respond in kind. As Elder Eyring has observed, "You are doing more good [as a teacher] than you know."

"Relationships are critical."

Envision this belief pulling you from behind the safety of the podium and thrusting you into the lives of your students. The power of this belief comes in turning you from notes to relationships, from presenting to teaching, from low risk to high risk, from detachment to dynamic interaction. Teaching is by definition a human affair. You are not a teacher; you are a *person* who teaches. Students cannot separate your humanness from your message; in fact, your humanness *is* the message. The way to learning is through relationships. You enter into relationships as you enter the room to teach. Teachers in the Church do not normally attend to the power of relationships. While courtesy and respect are practiced by most, few sense the power of teaching *through* relationships. In my interviews with teachers, most attest to the value of "relating well to your students" but minimize relationships by focusing on content once they are in the classroom.

Summary

Acknowledged or hidden, our personal beliefs powerfully influence our teaching: Some liberate while others imprison. Some lead to sappy and impotent practices, others to authentic improvement. The task is to honestly explore our beliefs, revising and substituting, thus freeing ourselves to try out changes in our teaching.

[1] Dan Lortie. *School Teacher: A Sociological Study*. Chicago: The University of Chicago, 1975, p. 79.

CHAPTER 7

GOSPEL STUDY

This chapter will illustrate how the consequences of insufficient Gospel study are reflected in our teaching. We will then show, on the other hand, how ongoing study provides the foundation for strong lessons.

A Debriefing

Listen in on a conversation between roommates Brett and Scott; Scott is uneasy about a priesthood lesson he has just taught:

> "You figure it out. I read over the lesson four or five times, think about it off and on for a day-and-a-half, select quotes I think the guys will relate to, pray for the Spirit, put in a scripture or two—and end up giving a ho-hum lesson. It has no power."

> "Maybe your well was dry—no water to be drawn."

> "Uh—try me again."

> "No flesh on the bones."

> "Enough philosophical romance. Just tell me what went wrong—you're sitting in that class."

> "I'm trying to. Pick a male religion professor at BYU who teaches latter-day Church history. Have him give your priesthood lesson. What's the difference?"

> "Be serious!"

> "No, tell me."

"Well, he'd be more credible—more believable—the guys would sit up and listen. He'd have great confidence when he talks about Joseph F. Smith, obviously, he teaches about him every day. He'd have plenty at his fingertips—Joseph's background, conversion, leadership, attitudes, personal struggles—I mean he'd have a veritable storehouse to call on! I don't know—he'd just come across so different to these guys. He'd command their attention—there'd be a presence about him—I'd come off threadbare by comparison. It's kind of like quality—you can't define it but can tell when it's not there."

"Well, yes, this discussion helps me tons. What am I supposed to do? I'm a student carrying sixteen hours—not a religion professor—scrambling to have *something* for these guys each Sunday. There's no more in me."

Another Comparison

For two years my wife and her friend have driven to Sandy each week to a religion class taught by an Institute teacher at the University of Utah. I have sat through a number of his classes on various subjects and have been impressed by his depth of understanding, his insights into the scriptures, and his ability to teach them. This year the course is Book of Mormon. Each week my wife returns with copious notes and with the excitement of new insights she has received. Coincidentally, I teach in the Stake Institute Program, and this year we too are studying The Book of Mormon. Gaile attends my classes as well. As a professional full-time Church teacher, he has paid the price for his facility in teaching The Book of Mormon; as a once-a-week, volunteer teacher, I have not. His lifetime of study shows in every lesson; my sporadic and piecemeal study also shows in every lesson. *There is no substitute for ongoing Gospel study.*

The fruits of ongoing, life-long preparation are exemplified in the secular world in the life of George Lincoln Burr (1857-1938), who taught history at Cornell for more than three decades:

[Frequently] he would be wrapped in the subject, oblivious of the books which were never once opened, to the chagrin of the student who helped him to carry them over and back. He discouraged all note taking and made it practically impossible. On the bookish days his comments would be too unsystematic to take down, and in the inspired hours the listener was too enthralled to write, even were he able to keep up with the two hundred words a minutes. Those lectures were works of art, symmetrical in structure, rich in diction, rhythmic in their periodic cadences. The notes which were occasionally gleaned by students give the impression of someone plucking a few gorgeous feathers from the plumage of a bird on the wing.[1]

Ongoing Gospel study differs from preparing next week's lesson. Your desires to search the scriptures and the words of modern prophets to understand the Lord's relationship to His children in general and to you in particular draw you into daily, or at least consistent, Gospel study. Your study is personal, for your own development.

Preparing to teach a particular lesson, on the other hand, requires focused effort in order to convey a suggested message. The purpose of this kind of study is to teach doctrine, introduce new insights and concepts, cause remembrance, support and build testimonies, invite students into the scriptures to learn for themselves—all in a teaching moment on a given day.

The natural tendency is to ignore the relationship between ongoing Gospel study and preparation of specific lessons from manuals. Realistically, when a person is called to teach, preparation of individual lessons unfortunately *becomes* one's ongoing study, constricting the power that comes from a broader foundation of Gospel understanding. Only ongoing study provides the credibility, power, authority, richness, and depth in teaching. *Your ongoing study, without your conscious thought, skillfully invades every lesson you teach.* Ever present in the wings are thoughts, understandings, insights, experiences of and lessons learned by people in the scriptures, each awaiting a cue from the Spirit to enter the stage.

Threadbare Lessons

Brett used this homespun metaphor in comparing his teaching to that of an experienced professor. Teachers are challenged in differentiating ordinary teaching from *real* teaching. Their diagnosis of ordinary teaching includes such statements as:

"Not enough preparation."

"Knows only what's in the lesson."

"Inadequate background."

"A feat any member of the class could perform with manual in hand."

"Same thing could be realized by simply reading the lesson."

"He throws in a personal story and scripture once in a while, but that's about it."

Thread-bare teaching leaves students feeling ho-hum, with only an occasional insight, not particularly inspired. Note this reaction by a student having sat through threadbare lessons:

"Another kind of pride and short-mindedness is seen when teachers try to make up for a lack of subject matter knowledge. I had seen the symptoms of shallow-knowledge teaching, but it had never before occurred to me what was going on. How many times have I sat through lessons that gave a 'broad range of superficial coverage,' or ones that were so 'tightly packaged' I hardly felt like I was allowed to breath through? Sadly, so many of our Church teachers think that highly-structured, lavishly polished lessons are the ideal; they are not aware that if they are prepared they don't even need to strive for that, it will come naturally. The teacher with deep understanding of the subject does not fear the inspired diversion, the unfinished lesson, or the unrelated question—but welcomes the Spirit of them. The need for power is lost in this, as motives are purely focused on *teaching* not *impressing*."

Ongoing Reconstruction

Consider the power generated from deeper Gospel study. The new curriculum admonishes us to "put more substance into instruction, emphasizing the scriptures and doctrinal teachings of latter-day prophets."[2]

At first thought, one might decide that threadbare lessons can be mended by greater specific preparation. This solution is only partly accurate: Specific preparation and elegant presentation are temporary patches at best. Ongoing study offers a stronger basis for reconstruction, as it affects preparation and presentation in a continuing way. Yet few select this long-term strategy. Carefully studying the scriptures, tracing cross references, and making notes requires time and can be put off, while next week's lesson demands immediate attention. Does disciplining oneself for ongoing study actually affect those demanding weekly lessons? Let me suggest a few benefits.

<u>You come to the lesson with a storehouse of parallel examples.</u>

Offering one example of a concept or principle may produce partial understanding, while including a second, related example often allows richer and more complete comprehension and application. Additionally, several examples of the same principle tend to deepen the student's conviction (testimony) of that principle. Ongoing study prepares you with a wide range of possibilities which surface at just the right moment. The internal conversation goes something like this: "It just now occurred to me that this situation is almost identical to the one I was reading about the other day in the 89th Section. It would be helpful to share." Note the following two parallel examples.

In ongoing study, you are presently working through Judges in the Old Testament, and the account of Samson's life has been sobering for you. An angel appeared to his mother saying, "For, lo, thou shalt conceive, and bear a son; and no razor shall come on his head: for the child shall be a Nazarite unto God from the womb; and he shall begin to deliver Israel out of the hands of the Philistines" (Judges 13:5). But Samson grew proud, strong willed, and lustful, and he ignored God's purpose for him. Finally succumbing to Delilah's plea to know the secret of his strength, "He told her all his heart, and said unto her, There hath not come a razor upon mine head; for I have been a Nazarite unto God from my mother's womb: if I be shaven, then my strength will go from me, and I shall become weak, and be like any other man" (Judges 16:17). Later, blind and standing between two pillars supporting a house full of men and women, he pled with the Lord, "Let me die with the Philistines. And he bowed himself with all his might; and the house fell upon the lords, and upon all the people that were therein. So the dead which he slew at his death were more than they which he slew in life" (Judges 16:30). In pondering this man's life you are reminded of a statement by C. S. Lewis quoted by another teacher to this effect: "Those who refuse to become God's sons become God's tools." When Samson became "like any other man," he ceased to be a son of God and became God's tool in destroying the Philistines.

Concurrently, you are teaching a class on The Book of Mormon and, while studying Second Nephi, the class arrives at the separation of the family into two groups. In Chapter 5: 21 you focus on this statement: "That they [Lamanites] might not be enticing unto my people [Nephites] the Lord did cause a skin of blackness to come upon them." Then in verse 25 you read, "They [Lamanites] shall be a scourge unto thy seed, to stir them up in remembrance of me." Into your mind comes the life of Samson, as well as the statement by C.S. Lewis that you have associated with it. Bringing in this example of the Lord using Samson as a tool—just as he did with the Lamanites in the lesson you are now preparing—offers students greater richness and credibility in thinking about sons and tools and, more importantly, about the inevitability of God's purposes.

Consider a second example: You are teaching Book of Mormon and come to 1 Nephi 2. The Lord blesses Nephi who, unlike his brothers Laman and Lemuel, has sought Him in faith and "with lowliness of heart"(vs 19). The Lord assures Nephi, "And insomuch as thy brethren shall rebel against thee, they shall be cut off from the presence of the Lord. And insomuch as thou shalt keep my commandments, thou shalt be made a ruler and teacher over thy brethren" (vs 21-22). From ongoing study you have in your mind the parallel example of Joseph, who was sold into Egypt by his brothers and who later became their ruler. Combining the second example with the first offers students a more convincing, multifaceted view of the Lord using righteous people to lead. Further, you recall the relationship of Joseph and Hyrum, a contrasting situation in which when the younger is chosen as the leader the older remains faithful and righteous. This third example opens new thinking about birthright, selection and righteousness.

<u>You achieve deeper, additional and alternative insights into the lesson.</u>

Ongoing study has taught you to "dig deeper": to look for alternative and more inclusive meanings; to interpret, extend, and create metaphor. This pondering skill, developed with continued practice, helps you go below the surface, see different sides, ask thoughtful questions about purpose, and see relationships. You transport this pondering skill to the preparation of next week's lesson. Here are several examples:

At first reading, Mosiah 4:14 sounds like a commandment: "And ye will not suffer your children that they go hungry, or naked; neither will ye suffer that they transgress the laws of God, and fight and quarrel one with another, and serve the devil, who is the master of sin, or who is the evil spirit which hath been spoken of by our fathers, he being an enemy to all righteousness." But when you study the relationship of this scripture to earlier verses, you realize that these statements can be viewed as a promise that is fulfilled when you "humble yourselves even in the depths of humility," "calling on the name of the Lord daily," and "standing steadfastly in the faith." The Lord affirms, And behold, I say unto you that *if ye do this* [italics added] ye shall always rejoice . . . And ye shall not have a mind to injure one another" (11-14).

At first reading of 3 Nephi 27:13 appears to be a straightforward declaration of the Savior: "Behold I have given unto you my gospel, and this is the gospel which I have given unto you—that I came into the world to do the will of my Father, because my Father sent me." But further study reveals an interesting possibility if emphasis is placed on particular words: "This is the gospel which *I* have given unto you—that *I* came into the world to do the will of my Father, because my Father sent *me*." Another personage enters the picture: Satan.

In 1 Nephi 4:10-17 we see the process of human reason and the workings of by the Spirit. Nephi is constrained by the Spirit to kill Laban, an instruction from with he immediately recoils. Then the Spirit helps him reason about this act:

> "And the Spirit said unto me: Behold (1) the Lord hath delivered him into thy hands. Yea, and I also knew that he (2) had sought to take away my own life; yea and (3) he would not hearken unto the commandments of the Lord; and (4) he had also taken away our property.... Behold (5) the Lord slayeth the wicked to bring for his righteous purposes. (6) It is better that one man should perish than that a nation should dwindle and perish in unbelief. And now, when I, Nephi, had heard these words of the Lord which he spake unto me in the wilderness, saying: (7) Inasmuch as thy seed shall keep my commandments, they shall prosper in the land of promise. Yea, (8) and I also thought that they could not keep the commandments of the Lord according to the law of Moses, save they should have the law. And I knew that the law was engraven upon the plates of brass. (9) And again [third time], I knew that the Lord had delivered Laban into my hands for this cause.... Therefore I did obey the voice of the Spirit, and took Laban by the hair of the head, and I smote off his head with his own sword."

Nephi studied this situation out in his mind as the Spirit continued to prompt him.

<u>You come to the lesson with skill in drawing applications to modern life.</u>
Through ongoing study you regularly ask, "How can this apply to my own life here and now?" Practice in deriving applications develops a skill you carry into the preparation of each lesson. Teaching comes alive and is powerful when students connect principles to their own lives. Additionally, the storied lives of people in the scriptures have powerful effects on students. They see themselves, their strengths and weaknesses, in these scriptural lives. You should approach individual lessons with the intention of making applications. Following are several examples:

Jacob³ began to realize the importance of record keeping: "But whatsoever things we write upon anything save it be upon plates must perish and vanish away; but we can write a few words upon plates, which will give our children, and also our beloved brethren, a small degree of knowledge concerning us, or concerning their fathers—Now in this thing we do rejoice; and we labor diligently to engraven these words upon plates, hoping that our beloved brethren and our children will receive them with thankful hearts, and look upon them that they may learn with joy and not with sorrow, neither with contempt, concerning their first parents."

As you teach this scripture, you can help your students understand that their personal journals can provide their children with insights into their parents' lives—so they may remember their parents with thankful hearts rather than with contempt, and be encouraged to learn with joy rather than sorrow.

Laman and Lemuel were masters at murmuring, and perhaps when we view their overall context, we might find some justification. But as we explore this human trait in them and in ourselves, we discover two interesting aspects: "And thus Laman and Lemuel, being the eldest, did murmur against their father. And they did murmur because they knew not the dealings of that God who had created them."[4] When we fail to understand the purposes of God in our own lives, we are prone to murmur. As with Laman and Lemuel, our whining may be evidence that we are not living close enough to the Lord. Second, murmuring is a form of blaming: "And now it came to pass that after I, Nephi, had made an end of speaking to my brethren, behold they said unto me: Thou hast declared unto us hard things, more than we are able to bear."[5] Flaunting their wounds was an attempt to wound their brother. So it is with us. Claiming that others have hurt us is our way of punishing them. The scripture can also be applied to teach that when we experience great pain from chastisement, we are usually in the wrong.

<u>You come to your lessons with greater confidence and credibility.</u>
We have all experienced the contrast in confidence we feel when our preparation is exhaustive or skimpy—and we know our

students can feel it as well. Coming to class with a much wider Gospel understanding gained over years of ongoing study engenders even more confidence: confidence that arises from substance not puffery. Could this be in part the kind of confidence the Lord referred to while talking with Joseph Smith: "Then shall they confidence wax strong in the presence of God."[6] In the minds of students, credibility comes from teacher expertise, not from exaggeration, preaching, self-proclaiming or superficiality. Genuine expertise creates in the teacher neither bulldozing overconfidence nor syrupy humility, but simple, solid power.

<u>You come to your lessons with greater humility.</u>

When the heart is right, ongoing study makes us teachable, promotes a sense of awe for God's purposes and for His love for mankind. Truman Madsen, a lifelong student of the Prophet Joseph, conveys this humility as he describes the Prophet's personality and character:

> "I begin with that [Sidney B. Sperry's claim that no man in this generation could possibly know as much about the scriptures as did the Prophet Joseph Smith] because a feeling constantly recurs as one studies the life of Joseph Smith. You can be so impressed and overcome with glimpses that you say, 'Nothing good that I could learn of him would be surprising.' And then you become surprised. There is always more. It takes deep to comprehend deep, and I often wonder if any of us have the depth to fully comprehend this man."[7]

Some Suggestions

We all hear and respond in varying degrees to council from prophets, seers and revelators to spend more time in Gospel study. Our meetings brim with testimony of the fruits from Gospel study– and the desire to do more of it. Many seek for regular periods of uninterrupted personal study. But Church callings demand time and energy. With families, quantity of time is important as well as quality of time. More than before, wives as well as husbands are in the workplace out of necessity rather than out of desire for luxury. Other voices call as well: community service, vacations, social commitments and responsibilities.

Ongoing study, to be effective, must become an oasis in our busy lives. It cannot be hurried, falsified, substituted, or made instrumental—it must become an end in itself, undertaken in for its own sake and for personal reasons. It represents a return to simplicity, order, life-long learning. Demanding as it may appear, ongoing Gospel study is most fruitful when conducted with regularity.

In the clutter of our lives, finding ourselves in "the thick of thin things," we can be hopeful about ongoing study. Like physical exercise, *any* Gospel study, independent of lesson preparation, is transmitted into your teaching. As intensity and duration of exercise increases, so do the benefits. Even pondering one or more verses a day, or studying 10-15 minutes every other day, or completing a chapter a week can make a difference. Regularity is more important than amount. Whatever the deposit, the bank account will grow. Following are several suggestions.

<u>Ongoing study is primarily for personal development; stockpiling is secondary.</u>

Let us examine an extreme case. Suppose that in your daily personal study everything you read or thought about was prefaced with the question "Could I use this in my teaching?" An *Ensign* article titled "Working Through Differences in Marriage" falls into your category of "Teaching family relations." A General Conference talk titled "Looking After the One" fits into your "Fulfilling your calling" category. In First Kings 1: 1-30, Bathsheba, with respect and skill, reminds David that he swore to place her son Solomon on the throne and that Adonijah, taking the throne upon himself, would be an unworthy ruler. This story is referenced in your "Power of women" file. Quite unintentionally, you build a wonderful repertoire of teaching materials, but you personally have remained unaffected by them. There is no question that calling upon stories and scriptures enriches your *teaching*—but far more impact occurs when your *teaching self* has been enriched by the additional insights. Note this student's observation about the teacher and the message:

> "I have also come to understand a great deal about what it really means to understand and prepare a subject for teaching. In truth, it

is not simply reading up on a subject and presenting it in a clear format for students to remember . . . it is much more than that—it is spiritual. We must care deeply about everything we teach, so deeply that it is in us, or we will never be able to teach anything at all."

The purpose of ongoing study is your own personal development; *in the process* you will acquire a storehouse of knowledge which will benefit students. Develop your own truths, then share them with others.

<u>Building a storehouse.</u>
With the primary purpose of ongoing study clearly in mind, we can consider the mechanics of handling the information gained from that study: the challenge of storage and retrieval, of accessing information when you need it for a lesson or teaching experience. A few teachers can read or think about an idea or principle, make it a personal truth, then call it back at a moment's notice in the middle of a lesson. Most of us need *some* way of bringing to our minds and hearts what we have read, thought about, and want to keep available.

Avoid the mistake of turning means into ends. I suffer from dallying with information-saving and retrieval programs. I load information in one version, try it out, reload into a later version, then change programs and repeat the process. Always on the horizon is that program which can handle all my needs: the teacher's Holy Grail. I contrive key words, tedious category headings, nifty retrieval routines. However, the information too often travels from its source to my computer without being routed through my mind or heart. Finally, I grudgingly acknowledged that my storehousing had become an end in itself, and I was derailing my initial purposes. (To ease my guilt, I later renamed this tinkering a "hobby.")

Keep it simple. Computers with their unmatched memory and flashy possibilities can be seductive, attracting us to become *less* efficient. I recall striding into our home one evening enthusiastic with the news that I had stumbled onto a program that would allow my wife instant access to any recipe in her possession. Further, she could sort by type, ingredients, or number of servings. For example, if she wanted a "chocolate" evening, up would come chocolate cakes, puddings, and other desserts. Or she could sort more specifically on "Chocolate Cakes" and find German Chocolate, Texas Chocolate and so forth. Not terribly impressed by my enthusiasm but still willing to listen, she asked, "How would I go about retrieving my recipe for German Chocolate Cake?" "Easy. You go downstairs, turn on the computer, boot up the program, select "Desserts," type in "Chocolate Cakes," then select "German Chocolate," and press "Print." Then came the hammer. "Well, that's nice. Will it be easier than walking over to my recipe box and pulling out the card that says German Chocolate Cake?" Since then, the use of sophisticated software programs has not been a regular topic of conversation.

If your filing system is too sophisticated, you will lose the advantages of rummaging through a variety of materials in search of that special story, quote or scripture. Searching forces you to review, to remember that forgotten quote. On the other hand, if it is too simple, your system will not permit ready access to material you want to use. Choice of filing systems must be related to personalities and individual abilities to recall. My wife remembers almost everything she reads and is efficient with a set of folders in a drawer; my recall is modest by comparison, so keywords in a software program are important. Some of my colleagues at school are compulsively organized, with filing systems that are impeccable; others have offices and filing drawers that suggest a recent bombing—but they know where to find everything they need.

A cardboard box sitting obtrusively near a desk represents a simple filing system. Everything you read or make notes on goes into the box. At least there are no conflicting files to worry about. (Some people with several filing cabinets, become exhausted trying to remember *which* cabinet received their neatly filed quote.) A further advantage is that the box requires snooping, and thus reviewing, every time that important quote or article is to be found. The disadvantage, of course, is that more efficiency is available.

Pendaflex folders will never go out of style: They are easy to use, versatile, and not terribly expensive. File drawers full of carefully labeled folders have a strong track record. You can place entire articles, short quotes, magazines, pictures, and even objects in a folder. Different colors and tab settings on the folders permit even the most sophisticated groupings.

Computer databases can handle large amounts of information. Many homes are equipped with computers, and software packages are becoming well within the range of most family budgets. An electronic 3" X 5" card file is simple and powerful. The major problem with databases is that they represent the "card catalogue" for your "library," and everything must be referenced. If you read an important article in the latest *Ensign,* you must create a new "card" referencing title, author, magazine, and location in your home. Though setting up the file is tedious, once material is entered you can call up a quote or article from your database instantaneously. Since you have taken the time to type up a quote on a "card," you can quickly memorize or print it and leave it with the lesson just given, yet still be able to locate it from your "catalogue." You can always return to this centralized place when you do not remember in which lesson you placed that quote or where that story finally ended up.

Finally, the Internet is being used both by the Church and by private companies to help Church members access a continually expanding repertoire of information: Conference talks, articles and books by General Authorities and other authors, and biographies are just a few excellent resources. Teachers can download so much material that the challenge becomes deciding what to exclude from one's storehouse. With such an explosion of sources and material, you need to keep yourself focused on the primary purpose of your ongoing study.

Thoughts and ideas dart into our minds at odd hours and in unpredicted settings: lying in bed floating in and out of sleep, getting ready for the day, waiting in line at the supermarket, driving home or on a trip, sitting through sacrament meeting—almost any place. For this reason, note pads distributed strategically throughout the house can be beneficial for capturing fleeting thoughts and concepts. Some of your best thinking will occur when you are not trying to think, and thoughts that go uncaptured are soon forgotten. *Jot things down,* then throw your slips of paper into a box to be later revisited, processed and, if appropriate, filed. Some of your deepest insights, your most relevant interpretations, your most startling discoveries of relationships come when the mind is not focused on them. Your mind relaxes and becomes hospitably open to new impressions during these unfocused times. We often need to stop consciously belaboring an idea or scripture in order for the spirit's gentle impressions to "enlighten our understanding." Recording then setting aside is a process which allows this wonderful phenomenon to work. And, when back on task, the Spirit often enters the picture: "As I pondered over these things which are written, the eyes of my understanding were opened, and the Spirit of the Lord rested upon me."[8]

<u>Engage in periodic review.</u>

One criticism leveled against database systems is that once your quotation has entered the dark recesses of the computer you may never again see it. Periodic review, thoughtfully pondering what you have already come to understand, contributes significantly to your depth as a teacher. Memory experts have found that much of what we call "forgetting" is nothing more than failure to move information into our long-term memory. We forget something because it was never in the memory in the first place: "I'm sorry, I forgot your name. Please remind me." Experts tell us to repeat the name, associate it with some aspect of the person, spell it, make a cartoon out of it—anything to get it into long-term memory. The same is true with information we come across and want to file away for later use. Reading over a quotation that is already familiar, reviewing a biblical account or revisiting an episode from Church history allows the Holy Ghost to more readily bring it to mind. Said a friend on one occasion, "The Holy Ghost must have something in there to work with." Reviewing, then, works not only to build your teaching self but to render the influence of the Holy Ghost more capable of blessing your students. Note how Elder John A. Widstoe put it many years ago:

> "There is great power in knowing, and the man who desires to become a great inspirational teacher will have to remember this doctrine and fill his mind with the subject that he is teaching. Then he will teach well, and God will speak through him; and to his own astonishment he will say words, he will speak truths that were not clear to him before."[9]

Conclusion

We see in the lives of our leaders and many others the fruits of ongoing Gospel study. Their personal understanding and convictions, as well as their clarity of thought, testify to their price evenly paid. So too will our teaching reflect our level of sacrifice. Take heart. Even small oblations will produce significant results.

[1] Roland H. Brinton on George Lincoln Burr. *Great Teachers*. New York: Vintage Books, 1946, p. 173.
[2] Instructions for Implementing Melchizedek Priesthood and Relief Society Curriculum, 1 January 1998. Modification of the Gospel study program for Melchizedek Priesthood and Relief Society.
[3] Jacob 4:2–3.
[4] 1 Nephi 2: 12.
[5] 1 Nephi 16:1.
[6] Doctrine and Covenants 121:45
[7] Truman G. Madsen. *Joseph Smith The Prophet*. Salt Lake City: Bookcraft, 1989, p. 17).
[8] D & C 138:11.
[9] *The Improvement Era*, August 1917, p. 901.

CHAPTER 8

PREPARING A LESSON

Introduction

In this chapter and the next we move toward the classroom and examine how the inner self plays out in these public aspects of teaching. Important to remember is that the inner self cannot be separated from the teaching self. Your teaching style, your response to questions and comments, and your relationship to students are all expressions of this inner self. Realize, as well, that as the inner self changes so also does its manifestation in the classroom.

In these next two chapters, I will also describe findings from my research and from my work with teachers and involvement with issues facing them. Where possible, I will offer suggestions for preparation and teaching.

Teacher Purposes

Always in our minds is the *ultimate* purpose behind our teaching: to invite souls unto Christ. This purpose is a rudder gently guiding the course of the lesson. When this rudder is abandoned in the interest and excitement of a lesser purpose, the class veers off course and the power of our teaching is diminished. Keeping a hand on the rudder can be difficult if a teacher is preoccupied with his or her own performance. We lose sight of the students and of our responsibility to them as we focus on ourselves. This shift in attention is revealed in the following two conversations:

First conversation:
> "How do you gauge your success today?" (What criteria did you use?)
> "Quite well. My lesson went rather smoothly. I couldn't cover everything I'd prepared, but I felt good about my overall presentation." (Teacher performance)

Second conversation:
> "How did your lesson go today?" (The criterion)

"I wanted more participation than I got. I had to rush to get to the video, and the kids became restless towards the end—but I felt I covered everything I wanted to." (Teacher performance)

Inadvertently, the means have become the ends with these two teachers: Success is gauged by "how well the lesson went" *in the eyes of the teacher.* Performance, delivery, and coverage have become criteria for success rather than *what is happening inside the student.* A polished lesson, wonderfully delivered, may provide relieving satisfaction to the teacher but do little to invite students to Christ. *A lesson should contribute to reflection and change on the part of the student.* If during a lesson we invite students to "come to value the power of prayer," and one or two reflect seriously on their praying habits, then the effort has been a success.

Our good intentions must be reasonable and controlled. How easy it is to become carried away in genuine eagerness—zeal—to lead our students to Christ. In our fervor we can easily abuse their agency, as we put all our energy into *driving* them to salvation! This kind of religious eagerness has no place in our teaching. As we keep a hand on the rudder, we bear testimony and offer our students a quiet invitation.

Lesson Manuals

From our leaders, the counsel we receive consistently is to teach the doctrine found in the scriptures and represented in the manuals. Here is a sample:

> "Members need not purchase additional references and commentaries to study or teach these chapters. The text provided in this book, accompanied by the scriptures, is sufficient for instruction."[1]

> "How will teachers be encouraged to stay with Brigham Young's words and not compromise his message with outside sources?"[2]

> "On the second and third Sundays, instructors should focus discussion on the principles and doctrines taught by

President Brigham Young in *Teachings of Presidents of the Church: Brigham Young*—rather than bringing in outside materials. The text provided in the manual, accompanied by the scriptures, is sufficient for instruction."[3]

"Because of the desire of general Church leaders to hold fast to the principle of agency, there may be times when you will not receive the detailed directions you might wish to have. That is when you have the opportunity to go to your knees and seek for inspiration and direction to know what is best. And when directions are very specific, you can be assured they are important and need to be followed."[4]

Now, from the trenches, here is a sample of comments about lesson manuals coming from ward-level teachers:

"Teachers should follow the lessons that are in the manual because they are written under inspiration."

"I get frustrated trying to cover all the lesson material in 40 minutes."

"I love the way lessons are so structured—they lead you every step of the way."

"I feel hemmed in by so much structure—I don't feel I can ever bring in any outside material."

"The rote questions we are supposed to ask are so elementary and simple-minded I refuse to use them."

"I know I'm supposed to select those parts most relevant to my class, but I feel guilty not covering everything."

"If I don't cover all seven chapters next Sunday we will not finish the Book of Mormon by the end of the year!"

In my interviews with teachers, I have found that they are overwhelmingly committed to teach from the manual and to follow the lessons as outlined, a trend that seems to have gained momentum over the past five years. Among these committed teachers are those who are grateful for detailed structure, but there are also those who desire greater flexibility. In actual practice, most teachers do *some* adapting based on their own interests and commitments and the context in which they find themselves.

Today's manuals set forth considerable structure for the teacher: purpose (objective), teacher preparation, scriptures, statements and stories to be given, step-by-step lesson sequence, questions to ask, types of responses to expect, and a life application. In a world-wide Church there is great diversity in Gospel scholarship, from shiny new members with fragile understandings and testimonies to seasoned veterans with life-long understandings and commitments. Understandable then, is the difficulty of the task of the writing committees, who end up gearing lesson manuals somewhere in the middle. Among inexperienced teachers, the degree of structure found in manuals gives much security; to seasoned teachers, questions in the manuals may appear painfully self-evident, and answers seem overly simplified. As well, experienced Church members may find the life application questions to be elementary and superficial. Those writing the manuals face the challenge of providing scaffolding for inexperienced members without holding back those who are ready for more advanced material.

My work with teachers in the Salt Lake City—Provo, Utah area, across neighboring states, and during Education Week may not accurately represent all teacher voices across a wider Church. But these teachers do vary in teaching experience, are grounded in their Gospel understanding, and are committed to their callings as teachers—qualities to which one would hope all teachers aspire. The following suggestions grow out of our work together.

Lesson Building

<u>Prayerfully study the lesson for your own understanding</u>.
First, seek to understand the doctrine and supporting material provided in the lesson: "Seek not to declare my word, but first

seek to obtain my word, and then shall your tongue be loosed; then, if you desire, you shall have my Spirit and my word, yea, the power of God unto the convincing of men." [5] Inspired adaptation occurs best when the teacher fully understands what should be taught.

<u>Understand your students and your context</u>.

The most common impediment teachers place before themselves is not lack of commitment, nor inadequate testimony, nor failure to follow the lesson material—nor even lack of preparation: It is an *unwitting insensitivity* to the needs of their students. Unintentional but not unavoidable, it is reflected in this popular rationalization: "I have the lesson I'm supposed to teach—I prepare it—and I give it."

To increase your sensitivity and awareness of your students, try passing out a sheet of paper and pencil and ask students for a three-minute description of themselves—their interests, passions, dislikes and expectations for the class. Ask them to identify one thing that affects the way they learn the Gospel.

As you later review these responses, think of each of your students as wearing a pair of glasses through which he or she will view your lesson. The lenses are tinted in accordance with each student's level of understanding, needs, strength of faith and testimony, and unique interests and background. Borrow a representative pair, put them on, and return to the lesson. Amazing—a veritable Urim and Thummim! You can see the lesson *from the students' perspective*—and you can respond accordingly.

Understand, also, the context in which you are teaching. Study these descriptions to better understand your students' Gospel understanding, their testimonies, and especially their attitudes, orientations and personal views of the world. A group of teenagers living in a rural community will have different interests, ambitions, and background experiences than a group of teens living in an urban setting. Recently-baptized members will think differently than those who have been members of the Church all their lives. Hispanic members will come with different cultures and customs than will African Americans.

Adapt the lesson purpose to your students and their context.
Unwitting insensitivity begins when teachers ignore purpose. Recall the High Priest instructor who admonished the grandfathers to go ahead and have children while becoming financially stable. Had he thoughtfully considered the purpose of his lesson, he would have realized that the purpose published in the manual was not appropriate for his group. He might have substituted something like "High Priests will consider ways of helping married children and grandchildren balance their desires for material things with family needs."

Only as you come to understand the nature of your students will you be able to answer this question: "How can I adapt this purpose to *best* meet the spiritual needs of these students?" ("It is my *responsibility* to do so.") Suppose your lesson has the following stated purpose: Each young woman will understand the value of being dependable. Seven girls are in your Beehive class. You know their lives. Five of the seven are already wonderfully dependable. You realize this purpose needs to be altered somewhat to be more valuable. So you ask this question: "How can I revise this purpose to better help these girls in this general area of dependability?" Your reflecting goes as follows: These girls are dependable in both Church and school responsibilities, but I suspect less so in their homes. These are, after all, teenage girls on their way to adulthood. I can better help them grow with a somewhat different purpose: These girls will see how making their beds each morning and cleaning their rooms once a week will improve their spirituality.

The larger context behind specific lesson purposes.
Following is a random sample of lesson purposes taken from the 1999 *Book of Mormon Gospel Doctrine Teacher's Manual*:

> To help class members understand Nephi's vision of the future and how the warnings and promises in it apply to us today.

> To help class members strengthen their testimonies of the Prophet Joseph Smith and to encourage them to find happiness through trusting in the Lord and keeping His commandments.

To help class members feel a greater desire to magnify their callings, be chaste, and invite others to come unto Christ.

To inspire class members to follow the examples of the sons of Mosiah by sharing the gospel and ministering to others.

All of these purposes—including that for the Beehive girls—invite people toward Christ: encourage students to become Christlike in attributes and to promote the salvation of others—thereby working out their own salvation as well. Surprising as it may seem, *if you hold the larger purpose in the back of your mind as you frame the single-lesson purpose each week, the purpose of each lesson takes on a greater significance to your students.* Thus the rudder guides you in some directions and not others; you will say some things and not others; you will handle questions and comments in one way and not another; you will treat students in one way and not another; you will stay on course and out of interesting but unproductive channels.

Allow the lesson purpose to guide your preparation.
As a purpose changes, the lesson itself changes. Your adapted purpose will serve you well *if you are willing to use it as you prepare your lesson.* It will guide you, focus your thinking, and keep you on the road of relevancy. With your revised purpose for teaching young girls about dependability, you spend time thinking about 12-13 year old girls' bedrooms; you think about the relationship between tidiness, organization and spirituality; you think about how routine builds character; and, you think about how keeping a clean room will affect life as a future homemaker.

As your heart turns towards these girls, you will feel a keener desire to make your lessons relevant to their lives. You will create a variety of ways to do this once you realize your responsibility to do so.

A review of lesson purposes
1. *Tailor your purpose.* Create the purpose for your particular context—this setting, these students, their needs, this lesson.
2. Frame this purpose not in terms of you but in terms of your students. Decide what, as a result of your teaching, *they* will understand, think about, appreciate, feel, resolve to do.

3. Force yourself to think about a specific purpose; write it down so it will be in front of you as you prepare.
4. Avoid overextension. Realistically, one or two purposes for a given lesson are all that can be taught for in a single session
5. Keep this purpose in mind as your prepare. Allow it to guide your thinking and your selection and/or exclusion of material.

<u>Gather and sort materials</u>

Ideally a teacher will study widely and accumulate a storehouse of material from which bits and pieces can be accessed *when and if needed.* But how difficult it is to resist pedagogical dumping: shoveling every last story, poem, scripture and statement into the mix! "If a little is good, more will be better" is a faulty mindset. If two scriptures make the point, we bludgeon it with four or five more. If one story is powerful, we feel compelled to use two. The *inclusion syndrome* is usually born of good intention: our urgent desire to lead people toward goodness, to increase inspiration, to build stronger testimonies, to bring everyone to the temple. Soul savers by nature, we forget that our anxiety can also drive souls away.

The purpose in gathering information, finding new sources and studying related material is to *provide background, not to increase the amount of lesson material.* With this caution, let us look at some important sources.

Scriptures. The Brethren regularly remind us, "Teach from the scriptures." Scriptures recount peoples' lives, their struggles, their triumphs, their relationships with others and with the Lord. From these accounts of God's dealings with His people, great truths emerge. People learn principles from stories more readily than from stating or reading principles. "Families can be together forever," though believable, takes on power when one shares in the poignancy of Father Lehi's life-long struggle with his children. "Our covenants keep us separate from the world" takes on meaning when we see how Samson, the Nazarite unto God, left the hills of Zorah and wandered down in the valley of Sorek after a Philistine woman. "Riches, power and passion corrupt" is a warning which takes on meaning through the lives of Saul, David and Soloman. Finally, "blessings are predicated on obedience" becomes realistic when we become Laman and Lemual standing in the middle of the Arabian Dessert staring at Nephi's broken bow and dreading to "return without food to our families, who were much fatigued, because of their journeying they did suffer much for the want of food."[6]

Through the lives and experiences of real people, the scriptures teach lessons. David brings corn, bread and cheeses to the Israelite camp in the Valley of Elah, arriving at the moment when the king is searching for a man of Israel to go out against Goliath. In offering to go, David is fitted with the cumbersome armor of Saul, but says, "I cannot go with these; for I have not proved them." Instead he will rely on the help of the Lord whom he has proven: "The Lord that delivered me out of the paw of the lion, and the paw of the bear, He will deliver me out of the hand of this Philistine."[7] David has learned in whom he can trust.

Single words and phrases are full of meanings as well: Those who filled the great and spacious building were in the *attitude* of mocking;[8] the *vain imaginations* of the children of men;[9] get thee into the *mountain* (and I will teach you);[10] *pondereth continually*;[11] they had become like unto *a flint*;[12] they shall not be ashamed that *wait* upon me.[13] Each of these words or phrases carries rich meaning and has life applications. For example, overt mocking seldom occurs, but an *attitude* is just as punishing—the looks, the comments, the patronizing. Similarly, *vain imaginations* helps class members think about dreams and fantasies that are selfish and unproductive, leading to pride.

Personal Experiences. As an experiment, share with your class a life experience of a Church leader and an experience from your own life; watch closely their reactions to both stories. The stories of our leaders are rich and powerful, but your own experiences may be more moving to your students. You are face to face with your class, the story is your own. Your personal experiences need not be spectacular, and they may not be common among members of your class. But they are experiences which have influenced your life—they contribute to your testimony of a Gospel principle or illustrate one of life's lessons as you have learned it. Herein lies their power.

A highlight experience in our high priest quorum was the Sunday when one member was asked to take an entire lesson period to share his life story. No one was distracted or sleepy! Brother H., bent with age, lined with experience, stood before our group. When barely a young man, he had been called to fight on Guam and Iwo Jima during World War II. "Dad died two weeks before I left. I had to leave my angel mother, who was now losing two men in her life. I didn't know what to do. I had so much respect for them. I decided to place my life in the hands of God. I had many experiences I'm writing down for my posterity." Brother H. went on to tell of the death and suffering surrounding the battlefield, of how in the midst of cross fire he kept thinking of his "angel mother." "That was what kept me going." This humble man, with calloused hands and soft heart, taught us that day. Woven in and out of the stories of such men and women one can hear testimony in success, failure, suffering and joy. We identify with human stories because we too are human. Our lives touch and teach each other. We witness authenticity, struggle, compassion, forgiveness, sensitivity, sorrow, and healing—and the compassion and love of the Savior for each of us.

Your journal provides a rich storehouse of resources for teaching. I have an entry for most days of my life, and though routine is boringly present, seldom a week passes without an episode that can be crafted into a teaching possibility. Since this section champions personal experiences, I will illustrate with three of my own.

President Hinckley is a man of both prayer and action, as evidenced throughout his biography. He prays as if everything depends on the Lord then works as if everything depends on him. Having always admired that disposition, I have sought to teach it in my classes, particularly within the Church. Delving into my life story for an episode to dramatize prayer and works, I came across the following:

My military service consisted of six months of active duty at Ft. Ord, California followed by 5 years of active reserve. Several days of basic training were spent on the hand-grenade range. Far-sighted designers realized that 18 year-old recruits coming from all walks of life would be hazardous on the rifle range and even more hazardous on the hand-grenade range! Anything can happen when a teenager, living his fantasy of Rambo in the jungles of Viet Nam, is handed a live grenade. On the range is a concrete wall behind which all recruits stand to hurl their miniature bombs onto an open field. On their side of the wall is a large cement culvert into which a live grenade can be kicked if it should be dropped after the pin is pulled—a safety pit. On this particular day another trainee and I had been assigned to unpack grenades from their cardboard cylinder cases. We held the bottom half of the cylinder with one hand and pulled off the top half with the other. Our openings took place over a four-foot-deep barrel, into which the cases would drop as the grenades were removed from their containers. Since handling these objects was dangerous, I had offered a silent prayer for the Lord's protection. About half way through our task, my companion pulled the top off a container with such force that the resulting suction pulled the grenade out, and it dropped into the barrel jarring the pin half way out. Not taking time for another prayer, I lunged half way into the barrel, grabbed the disputable grenade, and threw it into the safety pit. Luckily the pin was not far enough out for the grenade to explode once it was in the pit. Regaining my senses and re–playing the incident, I realized the seriousness of those few moments. My mind pondered: Should I have stepped back several steps (no time to run) and quickly prayed for the Lord's intervention, or did I do the right thing in answering my own prayer but placing myself in harm's way? This story could be a good entry point for discussing the Lord's hand in our work.

An example with different circumstances but some common elements took place many years before. I spent several summers as a young boy of 10 or 11 helping my uncle and grandfather on their sheep herd near Meeker and Craig, Colorado. One day the two announced that they would be off rounding up wild horses, and I was to stay with the sheep, moving them in the morning and keeping them out of the alfalfa. Our sheep wagon (tin covered with the stove pipe protruding from the roof) was atop a small mountain so that the sheep below could be kept in full view. This day was long and lonely, and as afternoon waned a thunderstorm arose. At that age I was terrified of lightning, especially since I had witnessed strikes over the course of the summer. The presence of that metal stove pipe, pointing skyward from the highest point in the area, made me more anxious. As the lightening and thunder claps became simultaneous and the rain came in buckets, my anxiety finally turned to panic, and I bolted from the camp, somehow thinking I could run to the nearest town, eight miles away. Out about 1/4 of a mile, winded, desperate, and thoroughly drenched, I heard a faint call. Stopping, I turned to see my uncle sitting on his horse beckoning me back to safety with his hat. I trudged back up the mountain, with tears and rainwater in streaming down my face. Some five years later, my grandfather placed his hands on my head and pronounced a patriarchal blessing. His daughter, my mother, had died when I was two-and-a-half years old. At one point in the blessing, he said that my mother, working within her sphere, was watching over me as occasion might require. Several times during my life I have clearly felt her protecting presence. Years later, I received a witness that that day when a 10 year-old boy was running down a mountain in a lightning storm was one of those times.

Out of small, less dramatic incidents lessons may come. One snowy night my wife Gaile was attending a religion class on the BYU campus and parked her car in the lot adjacent to the building that houses my office. The area of each parking stall is not large, just enough to accommodate a regular-sized sedan. Returning to her car after class, she opened her purse, took out a single key, and unlocked the door. As she stepped into the car, she felt the key slip out of her gloved hand and fall silently into two inches of snow. She searched the ground directly beneath her feet and alongside the car, then concluded that the key had to be under the car. Another car drove by, and the driver helped her by shining his headlights onto the snow under the car. The two of them combed every inch of that small space, but the key was simply not under the car. Gaile called me, I brought another key, we drove the car out of the stall, and again combed the entire area. But the key was not in the section that had been covered by the car. Discouraged, we gave up the search. By coincidence I happened to park in the same stall the next morning. I went into my office, got down on my knees, and asked for the Lord's help in finding the key—an insignificant request by all adult standards. I put on my coat, went out to the car, and knelt for a final look. Immediately I saw the shine of our metal key poking out from the snow—in the exact spot we had combed at least four times the night before. No other explanation could fit into my heart that day. Small episodes build testimonies.

Life experiences for teaching need not be limited to faith-promoting events. Daily routine often provides wonderful images from which principles can be explained. Consider, for example, the routine that takes place in a plane waiting for take off. The stewardess explains safety features of the aircraft and says something to the effect, "In the unlikely event of cabin pressure loss, an oxygen mask will drop down from your overhead compartment. If you are traveling with a child, put on your mask first." An adult is not able to help a child—or anybody else—if she herself is dizzy from oxygen deprivation. You think about this situation and realize an important welfare principle: We cannot help others until we ourselves are self-sufficient. It is not necessarily selfish to meet our own needs.

Sometimes "small" encounters become symbols of greater principles. I once conducted a temple recommend interview with William Edwards, one of the great financial minds of the Church, a man highly valued and of great service to President McKay. At the conclusion of the interview, Brother Edwards stood up and, pulling his hand from his pocket, inadvertently scattered a number of pennies on the floor. We both dropped to our knees to retrieve the money. I couldn't help thinking, "Imagine this. Here I am picking up pennies with one of the great financial minds of the church." "There has to be a lesson here," I blurted out. With a twinkle in his eye and the wisdom of a sage, he said, "There is—you get rich by saving pennies and living a frugal life." What an experience to share during a lesson on "living within your means."

A trip through a shopping mall may furnish us with many "signs of the times." At a mall not far from my home there is a store with the name "Adorn Me." When I see its pretentious sign, I'm reminded about the *me* generation, about the temptation to become self-centered, about so many young (and older) people who insist on wearing name-brand clothing as they desperately seek for peer validation. A lesson on the great and spacious building could easily begin with such a sign.

Personal experiences can also offer hints about the *types* of messages you might choose to give when the occasion arises. As a bishop I discovered how easy it is to accuse others with your tears and how many people become "victims" in order to punish others. When there is some choice in the lesson, one might choose "accepting responsibility for our feelings toward others." Similarly, another lesson topic was suggested when I was visited by a Laurel confessing a transgression. After listening to her and searching for spiritual counsel, I said, "Given the nature of this problem, I would like you to hold off taking the sacrament for a couple of months." Her startled reply was "Why? I've come in and confessed, haven't I—that was hard for me!" A bishop's talk with the youth might be focussed on "confession as *part* of repentance."

Metaphors. A metaphor is "a figure of speech in which a word or phrase that ordinarily designates one thing is used to designate another."[14] Thus in "All the world's a stage," the world is spoken of as if it were a stage. Scriptures are full of metaphorical language: Christ as the bridegroom; Christ as the living water; the cup of His fury; the rod of iron; the serpent; the feast of fat things. There are frequent references to clay and wine to illustrate things of the body and spirit. Saints are instructed to "put on thy beautiful garments" and to "shake thyself from the dust." Metaphors carry meaning to the student because they refer to things within his or her immediate experience. Because they are familiar and often represent objects in the real world, they can be powerful. For example, in Mosiah 3: 19, King Benjamin speaks of a process that "putteth off the natural man." Most people can easily visualize putting off clothing that may be soiled or inappropriate. Using metaphors in your teaching can help students construct and order meaning in their own thinking.

Stories. We hear thought-provoking stories which carry important meaning into peoples' lives. Some are apocryphal, others authentic; some are within a religious context, others are outside. Sometimes stories are best told without comment, inviting students to draw their own meanings. Here are two examples:

Consider the impact the following story might have on a group of Relief Society sisters who tended to be quick in judgement of others. A woman had just negotiated a lucrative out-of-town contract for her company. Prior to boarding her return flight, she decided to reward herself with an expensive package of gourmet cookies, a dozen to be exact, which she slipped into her basket purse as she headed down the concourse. Sitting with her book open, she hardly noticed the man next to her reading his newspaper. After a few moments he reached down, opened the package of cookies, and helped himself to one! Taken aback, the woman could only shrug and take one herself. Moments later, he reached down for a second cookie, without so much as "Thanks, that was very good. May I have another one?" or "Thank you for sharing." Feeling affronted but unsure whether to respond, she took another cookie and crunched it down. Without removing his eyes from the paper, he reached for yet another cookie. The blood rose into her cheeks. How rude! Angrily, she gulped down another cookie, not enjoying it at all. They continued alternating as her fury mounted. Finally, in shameless impudence, he took the last cookie, broke it in two, and handed her half! Then folding his paper and turning to her with a polite smile, he vanished towards his flight. Livid with rage, she sat paralyzed. The ensuing 30 minutes calmed her enough to hear the boarding announcement. Leaning down to retrieve her purse, she spotted her unopened package of gourmet cookies.

Ken Meyer, a soft-spoken youth leader with whom I once worked, was asked to give a three-minute talk to the Aaronic Priesthood during opening exercises. He told of his early life on the edge of the Arizona dessert. With a friend, he would venture out onto the dessert to catch snakes. One day they captured and brought home a menacingly large reptile and placed it in a home-made pen. Their practice was to feed the snakes live mice, one at a time. The first mouse they dropped into the pen was, in one deft move, instantly swallowed by the snake. A second mouse was dropped in, but nothing happened. Tiring after a while, the boys decided to return the next morning to see the two humps in the snake's body. To their horror, they discovered that during the night the second mouse had chewed a hole in the side of the snake the size of a quarter! Had this small mouse continued chewing away, the snake would have died. My friend sat down, leaving the wide-eyed deacons to draw their own moral.

<u>Cover less material deeply rather than more material superficially</u>.

Suppose the lesson manual recommends covering 1 Nephi, Chapters 1-7 in 40 minutes. To attempt this impossible feat, the teacher blazes superficially through the story, pausing forbearingly for a student comment here and there. The goal behind these large assignments is that students will (1) receive an overview of an entire book of scriptures by the end of the year and (2) have a taste of the material and thereby go home motivated to study these seven chapters on their own. Almost the opposite occurs. The superficial coverage of Lehi's travels and challenges, which students have heard many times before, does little to pique their interest. In contrast, when the teacher slows down and deepens the students' understanding of one aspect or segment in the journey in the wilderness, new insights arise which *do* motivate personal study.

<u>Prepare widely, then prayerfully select one or two ideas appropriate for your class</u>.

Read and ponder related background material: quotations, experiences, cross-referenced scriptures, stories. But forego the temptation to include everything you have studied, everything you consider important—resist stuffing your outline and thus overcrowding your lesson. Select one or two ideas, concepts, or principles that you think will *most* benefit your particular students on that particular day. This task will be easier if your primary aim is to bless students' lives; it will become excruciating if your goal is to present elegant well-polished lessons, or if you are presumptuous about how much students are willing and able to absorb.

<u>Create an outline</u>.

Creating an outline *is* the process of building a lesson. Even the most well read and spiritually confident person would never think of going before a class or audience without some sort of outline (in the head, on paper, in the manual) of his or her intentions. These "outlines" range from three or four points hastily scribbled on a napkin to painfully developed masterpieces or organization and detail. Outlines empower you to enact your preparations, navigate along a mostly preplanned course, and coordinate the subject with time allotted; above all, they serve as a security blanket. Sometimes they can seem constrictive; at other times they give us a scaffold to lean upon. A recurring problem among teachers is that the outline they have developed fails to fit the class they are teaching: Overly-tight outlines can stifle an especially thoughtful and conversational class, while overly loose ones are inadequate to curtail "off the wall" comments. Mostly, outlines suffer from inflexibility. They fail to allow for important departures, alternate routes, inspired digressions, reduced time due to prior "meetings that have run over."

Each of us needs to develop and use outlines that work for, not against us. Our individual personalities, teaching styles and intentions move us to create our own most functional outline.

<u>Make the outline flexible</u>.

Functional outlines are developed in many shapes and sizes; each of us has his or her own preference. The problem that usually surfaces is too much material—too detailed and too rigid. In my interviews with teachers, I have found two persistent explanations: "Well I want to be safe; I need to have enough material so I won't run out" and "There's so much I need to cover, and it's all so important I just try to get it all in." In both cases the inevitable result is racing through the outline *because that is what the outline calls for*.

We want outlines to guide rather than control us; developing a flexible-breathable-format is one solution. Here is a possibility. Take an 8" x 11" sheet of paper and clearly label your purpose or objective at the top. Next, draw a line vertically down the middle, dividing the sheet into two equal columns. Start out listing in the left column points or concepts you intend to address during the lesson. These may come from the manual or from a group of chapters in the scriptures. Resist making an impossibly long list; force yourself to be limited. Under each, introduce scriptures, stories, experiences or whatever will help carry the idea (or principle) into the minds and hearts of your students. But here also be realistic and controlled. These major ideas may change sequence, undergo revision, or be replaced as you continue ruminating over your lesson.

The right column is your safety net, your storehouse, your bin into which you can place any story, scripture, concept, thought, poem, or quotation you have uncovered in your ongoing study. The material on the right side is not cluttering up your outline but waiting in the reserve *in case* the Spirit or your instincts call for it. This material is not planned into your lesson, may never be used, but surrounds and undergirds what you are planning to say. This separation procedure keeps you from "stuffing" your lesson and blazing through it. With but two or three ideas on the left, there is room for discussion, inspired digression—silence for pondering. An example has been provided at the end of this chapter.

Allow for Incubation.

Teachers differ in their style of preparation. Some think about their lesson all week, then the night before sit down and put their thinking to paper; others write notes all week; still others create an outline immediately after the last lesson and "fill it in" during the week. Each style has it own reasons and its own justification: "My stress builds all week unless I sit down right away and rough out an outline," "My busy schedule and my anxiety to face the task keep me from preparing until the last possible minute," "I gather material all week and throw it and my thoughts together the night before," and "I read through the lesson once, shoot from the hip, and everything works out surprisingly well."

A helpful process is to let things simmer on the back burner—there is a better flavor at the end. In general, teachers seem to experience less stress and waste less energy by preparing a rough outline early and allowing incubation to occur. Once several ideas are down on paper, the mind tends to unconsciously revisit and develop them while occupied on the surface with other things. A new idea or different approach often emerges while one is going to sleep at night, mowing the lawn, or filling the dishwasher. Somehow the mind on its own seems to be on the lookout for "things I could use in my lesson," even though conscious preparation has been set aside. Innocently thumbing through the *Reader's Digest*, listening to a talk, engaging in a casual conversation, reading a scripture, listening to music—any of these may stimulate ideas relevant to an upcoming lesson. Give yourself enough time to allow the lesson to bloom on its own.

Revise then go with it!

Refraining from sawing sawdust is easier said than done. We all fuss over our lessons, making a change here, dropping a part there, adding a new idea—all with the idea of improving the message. But too much revising, especially in the later stages, may leave us haggard and second guessing our inspiration. Here is where ongoing preparation and faith come in: "I am flexibly prepared and the Spirit will guide me into and out of my outline."

Note from the following conversation the nagging anxiety in "not knowing whether you have done all you can do:"

"Just today I came across two more scriptures I'd like to somehow weave into my lesson."

"Your lesson sounded great as you shared it with me the other day—why change it?"

"Well, I keep getting new insights that are important."

"Seems to me all your earlier insights were important too."

"They are, but I can't decide which is the best approach to take on this."

"Maybe there is no one best approach. Any number would be helpful; why not just pick one and go with it?"

"Because I don't want students going away feeling I haven't done my best to teach them."

In my own teaching I frequently mull over an idea or scripture, then mull over it some more and revise my outline even as I walk into class! What I know in my bones (but often fail to acknowledge) is that no matter how I organize or sequence a message, students will make their own meaning out of it. They will bring their needs, testimonies and experience to the message, all of which are outside my control. Simply put, I cannot be that responsible for how my students react to my message.

Understandably, constant revision may be due not only to spiritual promptings but to our anxiety to do our very best in serving students. We saw sawdust for the right reasons. Still, much of it may be unnecessary since we have no control over how the Spirit will work on those who hear the message. Try creating an outline early and allowing it to simmer with frequent stirring. Later, give it your best revision and go with it!

---

[1]*Teachings of the Presidents of the Church: Brigham Young*, Introduction, p.v.

[2] *Ensign*, Jan 1998, p.52.
[3] "Improving Gospel Understanding through Study and Discussion" From the First Presidency and the Quorum of the Twelve Apostles. *Ensign*, 1999, February, p. 72.
[4] Michaelene Grassli. *Leadership: Insights on Leadership for Women.* 1996, p. 30.
[5] Doctrine and Covenants 121:11
[6] 1 Nephi 16: 18–19.
[7] 1 Samuel 17: 37, 39.
[8] 1 Nephi 8: 27.
[9] 1 Nephi 12: 18.
[10] 1 Nephi 17: 7.
[11] 2 Nephi 4:16.
[12] 2 Nephi 5:21.
[13] 2 Nephi 6:7.
[14] *The American Heritage Dictionary, Third Edition.*

Sample Outline

Purpose: Students will come to sense that much of our suffering is self-chosen.

Outline	Material in the Wings

1. Types of suffering.
  a. Physical.
    i. Illness.
    ii. Accidents.
  b. Emotional/psychological.
    i. Anxiety of unknown.
    ii. Feelings of insecurity.
    iii. Emotional yearnings.
    iv. Broken relationships.
  c. Spiritual.
    i. Sin.
    ii. Unforgivingness
2. Self chosen suffering.
  a. 2 Nephi 2:27
3. The Lord selects our refiner's fires.
  a. He knows us.
4. We also choose our refiner's fires.
  a. Savior's choices.
  b. Patriarchal blessings.
  c. What type do I need to grow?
	1. Relationship between suffering and accepting every church calling.
	2. Harboring of resentment.
	3. "Why me?" vs "What am I supposed to learn from this?"
	4. Will it soften or harden the heart?
	5. "Boils of Job"—Three questions:
	  How good a man is Job?
	  What bad things happened?
	  How does he react?
	  "Blessed the latter time of Job more than his beginning."
	6. Satan—What *can't* he take away?
	  Agency to be righteous.
	  Our trust that all things will work out for the good.
	  Our testimony of the resurrection.
	7. "Suffering is the Sweat of Salvation" (Elder Maxwell).
	8. "Righteous sorrow and suffering carve cavities in the soul that will become later reservoirs of joy" (Elder Maxwell).
	9. "With regard to human suffering ... there is no way in which the misery caused by misused agency could be removed without removing agency" (Elder Maxwell).
	10. "The decisions we make, individually and personally, become the fabric of our lives. That fabric will be beautiful or ugly according to the threads of which it is woven" (President Hinckley).

CHAPTER 9

TEACHING WITH THE SPIRIT

With a shiny new Ph.D. from Stanford, I accepted a faculty position at the University of Washington and moved my family to the Seattle area. Our first ward was small, agrarian, and loving, and we met in a very old building. I was called to be the Teacher Development Director—well suited to my graduate specialization in learning, specifically concept formation. Each week I extended the standard curriculum with knowledge from secular learning, always careful to end with specific suggestions for teaching. We went on interesting intellectual excursions during our time together: into public schools, through research on teaching and learning theory—lots of fun, I thought.

Every week without fail, Brother H. took a seat at the rear of the classroom. His wrinkled face, weathered hands, bent-over frame, and tattered suit revealed his age of 75 years. He sat expressionless; I never heard a question or comment from him. In fact, I wondered why he was even there and how I could possibly say anything that would benefit his tired soul. He never took notes. He never brought materials. He sat, listening in a kindly sort of way. We were of different generations, different lives.

One Sunday I gave what I considered a rather decent lesson, actually a good one. Students filed out, all except Brother H., my enigma. At last he ambled to the front of the room where I was gathering up materials, internally basking in what I considered my achievement. He paused, looking at me almost tenderly, and said, "That was an interesting lesson. Too bad you didn't have the Spirit with you." And he left. I was stunned! Then I felt defensiveness swelling within me.

I spent the afternoon walking aimlessly around our apartment. My wife was perplexed but left me alone in my private inquisition. Why would he say that? How would *he* know whether I had the Spirit? Was he privy to my private prayers, my thoughtful study, my honest intentions? As night came on, the questions were unraveling my soul. Was he right? Was he seeing something I could not see?

145

By morning the truth had found me. Soul at last teachable and emotions tender, I quietly promised the Lord that never again would I teach without earnestly seeking the Spirit—and I expressed gratitude for a bent-over saint who had eyes to see.

Scriptures, statements by General Authorities, and Church teaching materials are replete with admonitions to teach with the Spirit. Following is but a sample:

> And they shall observe the covenants and church articles to do them, and these shall be their teachings, as they [elders, priests and teachers of this Church] shall be directed by the Spirit. And the Spirit shall be given unto you by the prayer of faith; and if ye receive not the Spirit ye shall not teach. (D & C 42: 13-14).

> It is a Gospel teacher's privilege and duty to seek that level of discipleship where his or her teachings will be directed and endorsed by the Spirit rather than being rigidly selected and prearranged for personal convenience or qualifications. (Dallin H. Oaks, "Gospel Teaching." *Ensign*, November 1999, p. 80)

> Teachers and class members should seek the Spirit during the lesson. A person may teach profound truths, and class members may be engaged in stimulating discussions, but unless the Spirit is present, these things will not be powerfully impressed upon the soul. (*Church Handbook of Instructions*, Book 2: *Priesthood and Auxiliary Leaders.* 1998, 300.)

In each chapter I have suggested the workings of the Spirit in one's teaching: its endowment to and influence on the inner self, its invitation to repentance, its influence in benefitting students, its role in Gospel study and lesson preparation, and its increasing influence on decisions opened up through teacher awareness.

Teachers believe in the importance of teaching with the Spirit. We are assured by comments like the following: "Today, today—the Spirit was there today," "The Spirit literally left the room because of their attitude," and "One thing is clear—the Spirit was *not* there—my lesson fell flat." While the presence or absence of the Spirit is discernable by many teachers; others are not so sure: "I can't really tell—even though I pray for it" or "How am I supposed to know—what are the signs?"

Based on our interviews with both teachers and students, the following observations can be offered:

1. A teacher can feel the manifestations of the Spirit while teaching, yet if her students are out of tune they will experience no such feelings. The reverse also occurs.

2. The Spirit works differently with each teacher and differently with the same teacher on different occasions, supporting different aspects of the teaching experience: remembering what was planned, managing anxiety, offering the right comment to a difficult student, knowing which question to ask, discerning inner turmoil, "seeing the thick of thin things," sensing the class mood, establishing rapport, being relieved of defensiveness, experiencing a wave of compassion, pacing the lesson, including or excluding material on the spot, and of course, bearing a testimony of today's subject.

3. Teachers whose lives are in tune with the Lord, whose thoughts and actions are habitually uplifting and wholesome, have spiritual discernment that is unavailable to teachers who are entangled with worldly ambitions and values. Their radar is more sensitive, allowing them to identify what others fail to experience.

4. The Spirit can be present *and* absent during a lesson: felt specifically in a testimony, a story, a scripture or comment. Only infrequently does the Spirit remain discernably over the entire lesson.

5. With an occasional exception, the Spirit does not step in and compensate for lack of preparation; it cannot expand what is not there. Sadly, teachers often stop just short of their best endeavors, thus impeding the Spirit from doing its work. The Spirit flows in on those occasions when it can extend and magnify our best efforts.

6. Each student experiences the Spirit according to his or her own needs and desires. It uplifts, testifies, and provides insights, as it offers comfort, hope and assurance to the teacher in feelings and messages triggered by an event in the classroom. A student comes to the teacher afterward with heartfelt thanks: "You were talking directly to me today; you said just what I needed to hear."

Are there recurring signs that tell us when the Spirit is at work—or when it has fled? The surest, of course, are our feelings. In addition here are several more:

1. The teacher differentiates between what is interesting and what is important—and teaches what is important. Because instructional time is so brief, teaching which builds testimonies is at a premium. Unlike Seminary or Institute courses on The Book of Mormon or Bible, Church teachers have but 35-40 minutes once a week. Beyond time constraints, the Brethren have counseled to teach the saving truths in the scriptures. Gospel instruction is aimed at building testimonies and bringing people to Christ, at avoiding interesting but less soul-saving instruction, as shown in the following examples:

> First Nephi 8 recounts Lehi's dream. The teacher embarks on the question of whether dreams (in general) *must* come to pass or *can* come to pass. With 30 minutes elapsed, 5 remain to explore the message of the tree of life and its personal meaning to families.

> In 1 Nephi 16: 18-23, Nephi, out hunting with his brothers, breaks his metal bow. Several class members launch a discussion on why a metal bow would break (salt, moisture, erosion of metal). With the help of the teacher, the class finally arrives at a scientific explanation for the breaking of the bow. The remaining half of the period can now be devoted to the lessons of faith and obedience growing out of this incident.

2. The teacher is moored to the Savior and His teachings. Whatever the path, lessons have a way of leading back to His life, His example, and our relationship to Him.
3. The teacher is sensitive to the spiritual needs of individual students in the classroom. Even while distanced from the Spirit, teachers can with considerable skill identify students' interests and discern their physical and emotional needs; but discerning their spiritual development and hunger is more complex. Our spirits, nurtured and refined in Gospel light well before entering bodies, require a more sensitive form of discovery. When a student's spirit speaks or cries out, the teacher responds spiritually—not flippantly, humorously, confrontively, passionately, or even matter-of-factly—but as one spirit speaks to another.
4. The atmosphere is pervasively compassionate, not argumentative, adversarial, authoritarian or defensive. Whatever the doctrine, the question, the issue, the concern, the disagreement, the atmosphere is one of good will, hopefulness, caring.

Plainly, the best way for a teacher to obtain the Spirit in teaching is to enjoy its company daily. One cannot expect to be magnified by the Spirit on Sunday without working with the Spirit during the week. There should be no difference between spiritual life in and out of the classroom. Daily examination and repentance of the inner self will inevitably be expressed in one's teaching.

CHAPTER 10

THOSE WHO WORK WITH TEACHERS

The First Challenge: Commitment to Development

This chapter is written to those who are leaders responsible for teaching within organizations: bishops' counselors, priesthood and auxiliary heads, teacher improvement coordinators.

Your stewardship for the quality of teaching in your organization is not only heavy but challenging, especially with the recent Church emphasis on strengthening teaching. Teacher development is a particularly difficult assignment because teachers see their callings as matters of teaching, not development. However, teachers must come to see development as an integral part of their work in classrooms; they have two jobs to do: teach and develop as teachers. Too often we fail to distinguish between the *importance* of good teaching and the *development* of good teaching. We drive home importance and exclude development: "Well, I come away with my motor revved up, but I seldom learn how to put it in gear and move out." It is always easier to talk about importance than development since development requires a plan of action.

Fortunately, the Church Teacher Improvement Program—with direction and talks from General Authorities—is leading us toward development. In effect, these materials say to the teacher, "Here are the fundamentals of good teaching: things you can do to become a good teacher." Reading and listening, a teacher then tries to adapt these principles to his or her own teaching.

The Second Challenge: Adaptation

In studying preservice teachers preparing for teaching careers in public schools, I am confronted with a recurring phenomenon: Skills that teachers have learned tend to be "washed out" once teachers move into full-time classrooms—not all skills, but many. These teachers are marginally successful in adapting what they have learned in college to their individual classrooms. The context can be formidable! "I tried student-centered instruction with my low-achievers, and it was hopeless—they need far more structure"; "Pre–organizers were not much help to these high-achieving students, and the polynomial unit did not lend itself to using them"; "Low-profile intervention sure didn't work with this level of disruption!" These failures do not necessarily result from these teachers having learned false theories and skills, but from their inability to *adapt a skill to a particular context.*

The same challenge is faced by Church teachers. Fundamentals of effective teaching identified in Chapter 1 are not false. Indeed, their strength is attested in the scriptures and in talks by General Authorities—and it is supported by secular research. The problem is one of transfer (the secular term) or adaptation (the Church term) to a specific context. Consider again the summary of teaching principles from Chapter 1:

1. Prepare diligently and prayerfully.
2. Study the scriptures continually.
3. Teach with the Spirit.
4. Be humble.
5. Love those whom you teach.
6. Focus on the students, their needs and testimonies.
7. Be pure and live the Gospel.
8. Teach the doctrine of Christ from prescribed manuals and the scriptures.
9. Employ effective techniques (e.g. vary your methods, use visual aids, ask questions, involve class members through discussions, include relevant stories and object lessons, maintain eye contact, adapt lessons to class members).

Note that principles 1 through 8 need no adaptation; they are context free, to be employed by every teacher in every classroom. In contrast, Principle 9, which focuses exclusively on method, *does* require adaptation in each classroom and with each teacher. A class of experienced adults doesn't require as many object lessons as a class of ten-year-olds. For adults, objectification is often in the form of stories or experiences as compared to actual objects used in the younger classes. Finding stories relevant to a particular group is another example of adaptation. A story of a girl helping her father with haying may be less relevant to modern teenagers than a story about four girls on a hay ride or participating in a community service project. In-service lessons discuss both context-free principles (1-8) and techniques (9), but when discussing the latter, they often ignore context.

The second challenge, then, is not met by simply *encouraging* teachers to adapt their lessons to their students, to their own context. Teachers must be helped in making these adaptations.

The Leader's Role

First-Stage Instruction

The first challenge, a commitment to development, is approached through first-stage instruction: the formal training programs of the Church underscored with a motivation for *continuing development*. In calling a teacher, the leader explains that the role includes both teaching and developing. In setting apart a teacher, the priesthood leader blesses the person with a desire to improve, to grow in effectiveness, to continue developing. The entire program emphasizes a spirit of continuing development. As teachers experience these reinforced expectations of an expanded role, they begin to fulfill them.

The Basic Course, subsequent in-service meetings, special meetings, videos on teaching, and occasional classroom visits are all helpful resources for first-stage instruction. With these materials the focus is on *Principles of Teaching*. These are relatively short exposures, conducted away from the teacher's classroom—that teaching space where the teacher's life, the subject, and the students all come together in a dynamic relationship

Second-Stage Instruction

Second-stage instruction focuses on *what is happening in the teacher's classroom:* where adaptation is tried, where experimentation occurs, and where change is motivated and implemented through the influence of the Spirit. Change which develops naturally through classroom events is very powerful. In addition to being renewed, inspired and instructed from an in-service meeting, the teacher feels compelled to change by an awareness of events in her classroom. We turn now to the role of the leader in the teacher's development.

The second challenge, helping teachers learn to adapt, is addressed through bringing second-stage instruction into the teacher's classroom. The teacher becomes a student of his own teaching, as he himself studies it in his own classroom. This classroom study becomes a sturdy ladder against the wall of continuing development. Here the teacher attempts to adapt and adopt principles of teaching he has learned, often concurrently, through the Church program. But more occurs as we have seen throughout this book. Through simple information-gathering procedures, his awareness of events is expanded, and he changes, experiments, confirms and studies the terrain of his teaching. This study of himself within his own classroom, in community with the students and the subject, the excavation of new possibilities, is his second-stage instruction.

A metaphor may be helpful. The individual called for teacher-support communicates with the teacher: "Can I assist you as you study your teaching? If so, we might try a flashlight. As a team we can decide what kind of a flashlight to use and where it will be shone. In illuminating different aspects of your teaching, you will certainly be comforted with some and may want to make changes in others. I will be happy to look with you—pass on my observations—but any decisions are yours."

The teacher improvement coordinator, with other commitments, may or may not decide to serve as a support person. A small support team might be called within each organization. In the Relief Society, for example, the counselor responsible for teaching might work with one or two other women who are assigned to one of the teachers. Once the role of the teacher-support person is understood—not as evaluator but as illuminator—teachers enter more readily into a relationship. To be sure, some are intimidated at the thought; others refuse altogether. But many welcome the opportunity. Time is required for the teacher to gain confidence in the support person, so rotation is not advised. Success breeds success, and interest grows within an organization.

This second-stage instruction is intentionally loose, permitting any number of different configurations. The orientation is more important than specific mechanics. Going one-on-one in her own classroom with a person she can trust is a strong and viable configuration. Adjustments, corrections and wholesale change resulting from her expanded awareness are guided by an inner self—one undergoing periodic repentance.

Examples of "flashlights" a team might use were discussed in Chapter 4. We have discovered that teachers become very creative in obtaining information about what is happening in their classrooms and what is going on inside their students. There is no end to flashlight types once interest has been aroused.

AFTERWORD

We have no choice. We all teach pervasively—with our lives by example, with our voice by precept. We speak of "safety" to a five-year-old, model the importance of order and self-discipline to a teenager, act with respect for a spouse, show unconditional love to a grandchild. After mortality we teach in eternity. Surely we must strengthen what we will be doing forever.

This book has offered suggestions for strengthening our teaching in one arena: the Church classroom. But good teaching in this setting impacts good teaching in other settings—as it is in turn impacted by each additional teaching experience. As we continue to develop our inner selves—reflecting on teaching moments, achieving insights through prayer, reading, and further experience—we improve our teaching selves.

Gary Sykes, a thoughtful educator, has said, "Teaching is a relatively easy activity to do poorly—and a difficult activity to do well. The hallmark of excellence in teaching is not easy mastery but steady improvement." This educator has said further, "The enemy of masterful teaching is not incompetence but complacency." Achieving greater effectiveness is well within the potential of every Church teacher. You have the potential, the desire, the stewardship, and the support—your students await.

APPENDIX A

FORMS TO HELP YOU STUDY YOUR TEACHING

FORM 1

MY REACTIONS TO SPECIFIC THINGS
THE TEACHER SAYS OR DOES

Directions to the student: Leave this form sitting in front of you during our session today. As I say or do something, feel free to write down any reactions you have. For example, "When you <u>look directly</u> at me, I <u>pay more attention</u>."

When you _____, I _____

When you _____, I _____

When you _____, I _____

When you _____, I _____

When you _____, I _____

When you _____, I _____

When you _____, I _____

When you _____, I _____

When you _____, I _____

When you _____, I _____

(Please hand this to me on your way out. Thank you.)

FORM 2

MY THOUGHT PATTERNS DURING THE LESSON

Directions to the student: I am interested in your thinking during the time I teach—when you feel something is worth attending to and when it is not and you prefer to think about something else. Keep this form in front of you and every so often during the lesson I will write a number on the board, for example, "4." Simply make a check whether you are "tuned in" or "tuned out" of the lesson at that point in time. Make your check opposite number 4. Do the same for each number I write.

The Number	Tuned in	Tuned out
1		
2		
3		
4		
5		
6		
7		
8		
9		
10		
11		
12		
13		
14		

FORM 2 (PROCESSING)

To the teacher:

Have a tape recorder playing during your teaching. Each time you write a number on the board (or you can merely pause and say the number) make sure the tape recorder picks it up. Later, tally all the check marks opposite number 1, those "tuned in" and those "tuned out." Repeat the process for each number. Then with the summary before you, replay the tape. When you come to number 1, note what you were saying or doing and the pattern of student responses. Do the same for number 2 and so forth. You synchronize your comments with student responses. This activity tells you what parts of the lesson students tended to "tune in" and what parts they tended to "tune out." For example, when you tell a personal experience, perhaps most "tune in"; on the other hand, when you read through a series of scriptures, perhaps the majority "tune out".

FORM 3

MY REFLECTIONS ABOUT MYSELF

Directions to the student: This is only a five-minute writing exercise to help the teacher better understand his or her teaching. Would you write briefly to these two questions:

1.   What happens in class that opens up my learning?

2.   What happens in class that tends to close down my learning?

FORM 4

THE TAPE RECORDER

To the teacher:

Take a tape recorder into class, place it on the desk near your voice, turn it on and go about your teaching. When students ask about it, simply say "I brought it in to listen to my voice as I teach." Later, listen to the tape and write your responses to the following questions:

1. What is happening in my teaching?

2. How are my students reacting to various parts of the lesson?

3. How are they reacting to me?

4. What recommendations do I make to myself?